W9-BHO-809

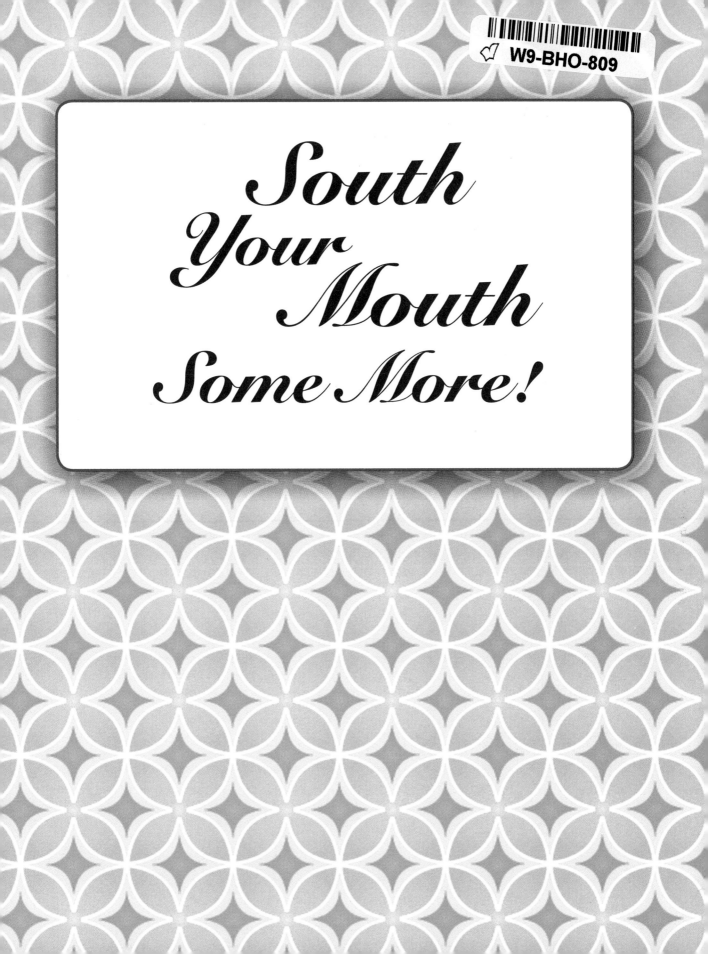

South Your Mouth Some More!

South Your Mouth Some More!

More Southern Recipes and Down-Home Humor from your Favorite Southern Cook!

Mandy Rivers

QUAIL RIDGE PRESS

Preserving America's Food Heritage

For my friends.

"I thank the Lord for the people I have found."
–Sir Elton John
"Mona Lisas & Mad Hatters"

Copyright ©2016 by Mandy Rivers

All rights reserved.
No part of this book may be reproduced in any form
without written permission from the publishers.

Library of Congress Cataloging-in-Publication Data

Names: Rivers, Mandy, author.
Title: South your mouth some more / by Mandy Rivers.
Description: Brandon, MS : Quail Ridge Press, [2016] | Includes index.
Identifiers: LCCN 2016020929 | ISBN 9781938879180
Subjects: LCSH: Cooking, American--Southern style. | LCGFT: Cookbooks.
Classification: LCC TX715.2.S68 R58 2016 | DDC 641.5975--dc23
LC record available at https://lccn.loc.gov/2016020929

First edition: October 2016

On the cover: Buttermilk Ranch Roasted Chicken with Potatoes, page 94
Food photography by Mandy Rivers

ISBN 978-1-938879-18-0
Manufactured in the United States of America

QUAIL RIDGE PRESS
P. O. Box 123 • Brandon, MS 39043 • 1-800-343-1583
info@quailridge.com • www.quailridge.com

Contents

Acknowledgments

My life is insanely busy and crazy! I love it, and I wouldn't trade a minute of my hectic schedule for anything different. But what's true is, if I didn't have the support system I have, there is no way in the world I could manage everything.

Without the help of Terresa Sullivan and Cyndi Clark at Quail Ridge Press, I would have buried my head in the sand and given up on trying to write this book this year. They kept me going, and because of that and the trust I have in them, we made it happen.

Without the help of my parents and friends, I wouldn't have made it to every one of the kids' games, practices, and competitions. Thank you Mom and Dad for all the pick-ups and drop-offs and uniform wrangling and bat-bag fetching. Thank you for always, always, ALWAYS being there for my babies. You are the best grandparents on the planet. Thank you, Cindy and Crystal, for playing taxi and doing it with a smile and a kind word.

And without my incredible husband, none of this would matter anyway. God blessed me with a man who makes me laugh every single day, who loves his children with his whole self, who is the piece of the puzzle that makes everything complete, and who I am so insanely grateful for.

I suppose this is the section I should acknowledge professionals like food stylists and publicists, photographers, culinary instructors, and chefs—but I don't have any of those. I have my village of friends and family, and for them, I am so grateful.

Preface

I used to think my dream was to be a bigtime TV personality on one of the cooking networks. I mean, how else does a recipe creator and food blogger define success? I even had a taste of it when Food Network asked me to be a cast member of the premiere season of *America's Best Cook*. Being able to say Food Network crowned me as "one of the best cooks in America" was a pretty big deal! I mean, I want that carved on my tombstone when I leave this earth.

After filming the show, I came home still believing that being on TV was the only way to define my success. I kept creating recipes, blogging, and even published my first cookbook—but still, I clung to the notion that I couldn't consider myself successful until I had my own television show.

Then one day I got The Call—the opportunity I'd dreamed of my entire life. I was asked to join the cast of *Food Network Star*. You know that show? That's the one where you win your very own TV show! This was it—this was my chance!

I jumped for joy and feverishly went about getting my ducks in a row to spend the next several months in Los Angeles. As I was sitting at my desk signing the contracts, a feeling stronger than anything I'd ever felt before struck me just as hard as if someone had walloped me in the head with a boat paddle. That overwhelming feeling was, I could not go. I simply could not leave my children and husband for that length of time. Ever. Never ever. Never never NEVER!

THEY are my success. They are what define me. I am a mother and I am a wife, and those two roles have given me more happiness than anything else ever could.

So I did something I never thought I'd do. I politely and humbly declined the invitation to go chase my dream. And I had to do it again when they called and asked me to be on the show the following year, too. (It wasn't any easier the second time.)

I hope I get another chance someday—when my babies are grown, and my love and I can head off into the sunset to chase my dream on the golden coast.

I tell you all this because these events not only helped me realize what was most important to me, but because it also helped me appreciate all of the many blessings I already have. I have the best of everything. I get to continue writing recipes for my blog and books while staying right here in little ole Lexington, South Carolina, loving on my family who make me so incredibly happy. What more could a gal ask for?

Thank you so much for taking this "AH-MAZE-ING" journey with me!

Mandy

Party Shrimp, page 26

Beverages & Appetizers

Have you noticed what a comeback retro recipes are making these days? Especially appetizer recipes. I think food bloggers have a lot to do with it, actually. We all dig into our family recipes, many of which our mamas made. And at my age, that puts a big chunk of my mother's recipe collection slap-dab in the 70's, like this Hot Chicken Salad.

"Baby Makes Three" Party Punch

1 (46-ounce) can pineapple juice

1 liter ginger ale

FOR BABY BOYS, ADD:

½ gallon (8 cups) blue fruit punch

½ gallon pineapple or lemon sherbet

FOR BABY GIRLS, ADD:

½ gallon (8 cups) pink lemonade

½ gallon raspberry sherbet

Refrigerate pineapple juice, ginger ale, and punch or lemonade overnight.

When ready to serve, mix pineapple juice, ginger ale, and punch or lemonade together in a punch bowl. Add sherbet by scoops. Stir occasionally to mix sherbet into punch as it melts.

Makes 16 servings.

Refreshing Cucumber Water

I like to serve this alongside sweet tea at summer parties, because it's a great way to cool down and wet your whistle without a boatload of sugar!

1 gallon water

2 English cucumbers

1 lemon

Fill a gallon-size pitcher with water. Wash cucumbers and lemon; slice, and add to water. Refrigerate overnight or until ice-cold.

Makes 16 servings.

Tip:

Make a half batch ahead of time, and make ice cubes. Use the flavored ice cubes to keep your cucumber water cold, if serving outside.

Cucumber Grapefruit Fizz

I love Cucumber Water in the hot summertime. I also love grapefruits and gin. Like… I love it, love it. Grapefruits and gin go together like Bert and Ernie! So I decided to experiment a little. I first made this with tonic, but felt like it needed just a tad of sweetness in there, so I switched it up and used lemon-lime soda. Bingo! I've also made this with vodka, and it's delicious, too. Use whichever appeals to you most.

1 part fresh-squeezed pink or red grapefruit juice

1 part quality gin or vodka (or more to taste)

5–6 unpeeled pickling or English cucumber slices

1–2 thin grapefruit wedges

2 parts lemon-lime soda

Combine grapefruit juice, gin or vodka, cucumber slices, and grapefruit wedges in a tall glass, and stir well. Fill glass with ice, and top with soda. Stir once more, then serve.

Note:

THE BEST way to make these is to combine your gin or vodka with several cucumber slices, and keep it in the fridge. The alcohol will absorb the cucumber flavor and take it to whole new level.

Mandy's Mojitos

I love this recipe so much, I planted nothing but mint in one of my flower beds, so I'd never run out! Definitely use freshly squeezed lime juice—it makes them so much better!

1 cup water

¾ cup sugar

1 cup fresh mint leaves

1 cup fresh lime juice

1 cup rum

2 cups lemon-lime soda

Mint sprig and lime slices for garnish (optional)

Boil water and sugar in a small pan until sugar dissolves. Remove from heat, stir in mint leaves, and let rest until mixture cools to room temperature (even better after 2 hours). Remove and discard mint leaves. (You can do this ahead of time and refrigerate up to one week.)

When ready to serve, combine mint syrup, lime juice, rum, and lemon-lime soda. Stir well and serve over ice. Garnish with mint and lime, if desired.

Makes 6 servings.

Low Country Hurricane Punch

This is a close cousin to the New Orleans Hurricane with a big-batch recipe for entertaining guests Carolina style!

1 cup light rum

1 cup spiced rum

2 cups pineapple juice

1 cup orange juice

Juice of 2 limes

½ cup grenadine

Orange slices and maraschino cherries for garnish

Combine rums, juices, and grenadine in a 2-quart pitcher, and stir well. Affix a cherry on top of an orange slice with a toothpick to make a garnish.

Serve punch in a tall glass over ice with orange/cherry garnish perched on the rim.

Makes 6 servings.

Mandy's Mojitos

Slow Cooker Hot Cocoa

This big-batch recipe for hot cocoa would be absolutely fabulous to serve as a "hot cocoa bar," with all the possible trimmings: peppermint sticks, marshmallows, whipped cream, sprinkles, crushed peppermint candies, toffee bits, mini chocolate chips, peppermint Schnapps and Irish cream (for the big people), and anything else you can think of!

Making this in a slow cooker allows you a way to keep it warm without worrying about scorching or burning, but you can make this on the stove if you prefer.

¼ cup unsweetened cocoa powder

3–4 cups whole milk

1 (14-ounce) can sweetened condensed milk

1 teaspoon vanilla extract

Pinch of salt

Add cocoa to a cold slow cooker. Whisk in 3 cups milk until well combined. (You always want to add wet to dry, instead of dry to wet, to prevent clumping.)

Add sweetened condensed milk, vanilla, and salt, and mix well. Heat on HIGH until simmering, then add milk to taste. Return to a simmer, then reduce to WARM or LOW for serving.

You can double recipe if you're making this for a party or bigger crowd.

Store leftovers in the fridge up to one week, then reheat in the microwave.

Makes 8–10 servings.

Note:

I make this with only 3 cups of milk because I love a super-rich, luxurious hot cocoa, but Husband likes it better made with more milk. Start with 3 cups, then add milk to taste.

Homemade Sports Drink

Our kids are all athletes. God bless them. And God bless Husband, because they didn't get a lick of that athleticism from me. I took the same step aerobics class for two years, and still screwed up the steps and tripped over my own feet.

Since at least one someone in my house is practicing every night, that much sports drink hikes up the grocery bill. Plus, it's got all sorts of stuff in it that I can't even pronounce. And it's loaded with dyes, preservatives, unnecessary calories and high fructose corn syrup. Hmmmm. So I found out I could make my own homemade sports drink. And the kids love it. It's crazy cheap to make, AND I know exactly what's in it (and what's not). Holla! What they're actually drinking is mostly water.

Now, listen, I wouldn't even begin to claim to be an expert on any of this, so feel free to do your own research, and please consult your doctor if you have any health concerns.

1 cup citrus or cranberry juice (see options below)

3 cups water

1 tablespoon sugar (or to taste)

¼ teaspoon coarse-grain sea salt

Combine all ingredients, and stir well. My crew is fine with just one tablespoon of sugar, but feel free to add more to suit your taste. Cover, and refrigerate up to one week.

Makes 1 quart.

Juice Variations / Flavors:

Orange: fresh orange juice (juice from 3–4 oranges)

Cranberry: unsweetened cranberry juice

Ruby Red: fresh ruby red grapefruit juice

Lemon-Lime: Reduce amount of juice to ¾ cup fresh lemon and/or lime juice, and add a bit more sugar to cut the tartness.

Philly Cheesesteak Dip

14 Steak-umm sliced steaks (1 pound), frozen

1 large onion, finely diced

1 teaspoon black pepper

1 teaspoon garlic powder

2 teaspoons Worcestershire

2 (15-ounce) jars Cheez Whiz cheese dip

CROSTINI:

Hoagie rolls or baguettes or French bread

Olive oil

Salt and pepper to taste

Remove and discard wax paper dividers from steaks. Place steaks on a cutting board. Cut lengthwise into 1-inch strips. You'll probably have to do this with 4–5 steaks at a time unless you're Paul Bunyan. You have to keep these frozen; they're too delicate to work with when they're thawed.

Heat a large skillet over high heat. Add steak strips, onion, black pepper, and garlic powder, then cook until steak is cooked through, breaking the steak up as it cooks. Drain fat halfway through cooking so that the meat sears instead of boiling in the pan juices. Once steak is cooked through, drain again, if necessary.

Remove from heat, then add Worcestershire and Cheez Whiz. Stir until combined, then place in a small slow cooker. Heat on LOW until cheese is bubbly, then reduce heat to WARM until ready to serve. You can also heat this and keep warm in a small saucepan on the stove. Serve with Crostini or crackers or chips.

CROSTINI:

Slice hoagie rolls (or baguettes or French bread) into thin slices with a serrated knife. Brush with olive oil, then sprinkle with salt and pepper.

Arrange in a single layer on a baking sheet, and bake at 400° until lightly browned and crisp, about 5 minutes.

Tuscan Sausage Dip with White Beans and Spinach

1 onion, diced

1 pound hot Italian sausage (remove casings, if applicable)

4 garlic cloves, minced

½ teaspoon oregano

¼ teaspoon thyme

½ cup dry white wine

1 (8-ounce) package cream cheese, cubed

1 (6-ounce) package fresh spinach, chopped

½ teaspoon salt

1 (15-ounce) can Great Northern beans, drained

1 cup diced tomato

½ cup shredded Parmesan cheese

1 cup shredded mozzarella cheese

Cook onion and Italian sausage in a large skillet over medium-high heat until meat crumbles and is no longer pink. Drain.

Stir in garlic, oregano, and thyme; cook 1 minute. Stir in wine; cook 2 minutes or until liquid has almost completely evaporated.

Reduce heat to medium; add cream cheese. Cook and stir mixture until cream cheese is melted.

Stir in spinach and salt; cook 2 minutes or until spinach is slightly wilted. Gently stir in beans and tomato. Pour mixture into a 2-quart baking dish; sprinkle with cheeses.

Bake at 375° for 20 minutes or until golden brown. Serve with chips, crostini, or crackers.

Note:

You can use any type of white beans: navy, cannelloni, or Great Northern beans.

Red Salmon Spread

This is one of my very favorite spreads to make for parties! Mil (my mother-in-law) taught me how to make this. I add a little liquid smoke to mine, but other than that, this is pretty much her recipe.

I usually serve this with crackers, but if you really want a special treat, serve these on cucumber rounds. They are beautiful (the green and salmon colors are so pretty together), and the crisp cucumber is such a nice contrast to the rich salmon spread. Cut 2 English cucumbers into ¼-inch slices, then lay the slices out on paper towels for about 30 minutes to dry out a bit. Blot the tops of the cucumbers with dry paper towels (just to make sure there's no moisture left, or the salmon spread will slide right off those suckers). Top each cucumber round with salmon spread, then arrange on a platter. Boom! You are uptown now, y'all.

1 (8-ounce) package cream cheese, softened

¼ teaspoon liquid smoke (optional)

1 teaspoon prepared horseradish

¼ teaspoon salt

1 (15-ounce) can red salmon

1 small onion, finely diced (about ¾ cup)

Beat cream cheese, liquid smoke, horseradish, and salt with a wooden spoon (or with the paddle attachment of a stand mixer) until creamy and smooth.

Drain salmon, then remove and discard skin and bones. Stir salmon and onion into cream cheese mixture, and mix until well combined. Add more salt, liquid smoke, and/or horseradish to taste, if desired. Spoon into a serving bowl, then refrigerate spread until ready to serve. Serve with crackers or crudité.

Variation:

Sometimes I make a "salmon ball" by lining a round bowl with plastic wrap before adding the spread, refrigerating until firm, then shaping it into a perfect ball when I'm ready to serve.

Note:

Red salmon is a little more expensive, but it's SO much better than the pink. And by all means, if you have freshly cooked salmon, go right ahead and use it!

Red Salmon Spread

Your Favorite Beer Cheese

I love beer. And I loved beer before it was cool to like beer. Nowadays, everybody's on the beer bandwagon. I use Newcastle because it is, hands down, my mostest favoritest beer of ALL in the whole wide world. EVER. Times infinity. Use whichever beer you like best. The cheese is going to taste like the beer you use. And it will get stronger the longer is sets.

16 ounces Cheddar cheese

1 tablespoon Worcestershire

2 tablespoons Dijon mustard

½ teaspoon salt

½ teaspoon garlic powder

⅔ cup beer (approximately)

Cut cheese into cubes, and add to a food processor. Add Worcestershire, Dijon mustard, salt, and garlic powder, then pulse 8–10 times, or until cheese is finely chopped.

Starting with about ½ cup, slowly drizzle beer into food processor while it's running. Keep running food processor and drizzling in beer until the cheese reaches a spreadable consistency. I usually use right at ⅔ of a cup of beer, but the amount you need will have a lot to do with the firmness of the cheese you use.

Refrigerate until ready to use (up to 2 weeks). Serve with pretzels, crackers, or celery sticks.

Parmesan Spinach Balls

2 (10-ounce) packages frozen chopped spinach, thawed and drained

⅔ cup grated Parmesan cheese

1 (14-ounce) bag herb stuffing mix (such as Pepperidge Farms)

1 onion, finely diced

6 eggs, beaten

1 stick butter, melted

1 teaspoon salt

1 teaspoon garlic powder

Coat a large baking sheet with cooking spray, or line with parchment paper.

Combine all ingredients in a large mixing bowl, and stir until thoroughly combined. Roll spinach mixture into 1-inch balls, and place on prepared baking sheet.

Bake at 350° for 20 minutes, or until set and lightly browned. Serve immediately, or cool and freeze.

Makes approximately 50 balls.

Kielbasa Bites

2 pounds kielbasa or smoked sausage

1 cup apricot preserves

½ cup Dijon mustard

Cut kielbasa into 1-inch pieces; put in saucepan.

Combine apricot preserves and Dijon mustard in a small bowl, and whisk until smooth. Add preserves mixture to saucepan, and cook just until heated through. Serve immediately.

Christmas Cranberry Cheese Ball

Now, I made this with goat cheese because I love it—but if you're not a fan, you could absolutely substitute cream cheese for a milder taste. As far as cheese goes, I like it when it bites back a little, so me and goat cheese are old friends. The twangy cheese mixture goes perfectly with the sweet cranberries and woody pecans, and the whole thing just looks like Christmas on a plate! The green rosemary sprigs and red cranberries make for a very festive display, and would be the star of any holiday party cheese board!

8 ounces goat cheese or cream cheese, softened

8 ounces sharp white Cheddar, shredded

1 tablespoon milk

¼ teaspoon salt

½ cup chopped pecans

1 (5-ounce) bag dried cranberries (about 1½ cups)

Rosemary sprigs for garnish (optional)

Mix goat cheese or cream cheese with an electric mixer until smooth. Add Cheddar, milk, salt, and pecans, then continue mixing until well combined.

Line a small round bowl with plastic wrap, then spoon cheese mixture into bowl. Press cheese firmly into bowl. Bring plastic up and over top of cheese, and gather to shape cheese into a ball. Seal ball with more plastic, if necessary, to completely cover; refrigerate at least 4 hours. It's okay if it's kinda wonky at this point. Once it firms up, you will be able to easily shape it into a perfect ball.

When ready to serve, arrange rosemary sprigs on a serving plate (I arranged mine like a wreath); set aside. Pour cranberries into a pie plate, and separate any that might have stuck together; set aside.

Remove cheese ball (in plastic) from the bowl. Keeping cheese ball wrapped in the plastic, use your hands to shape into a ball. When the cheese ball is perfectly round, roll in cranberries, then set on rosemary sprigs. All of the cranberries won't stick when you roll the cheese ball in them. That's okay. Just piece them on until the cheese ball is nicely covered. Serve with assorted crackers.

Hot Chicken Salad

I was reminiscing one day, and started flipping through my mental recipe box of forgotten favorites. I don't know if this is a southern thing or if everyone made it, but it was huge in the 60's and 70's around here. I made this and took it over to Mama and Daddy's to snack on before we had Sunday dinner. I figured they would remember this, but both of them just blinked at me when I told them what it was. They'd either never had it or just didn't remember it. I spooned some on crackers for them to sample. And my daddy really took a liking to it. He's a hard sell. It's got to be something really special for him to keep coming back for more, so when he made his third trip back to the kitchen, I knew I had a good recipe! I'll bet if you added some pasta to it, it would make a great casserole!

3 chicken breasts, cooked and cubed

1 cup diced celery

1 cup slivered almonds

8 ounces shredded Cheddar or Swiss cheese (2 cups), or a combination

½ cup mayonnaise

½ cup sour cream

1 teaspoon thyme

1 teaspoon salt

½ teaspoon pepper

½ teaspoon garlic powder

½ teaspoon onion powder

2 cups crushed potato chips

Add chicken, celery, almonds, and cheese to a large bowl, and stir to combine; set aside.

Combine mayonnaise, sour cream, thyme, salt, pepper, garlic powder, and onion powder in a small bowl, and mix well. If you'd like yours to be extra creamy, add a heaping tablespoon more mayonnaise and sour cream. Add to chicken mixture, and stir until thoroughly combined.

Lightly spray a shallow 2-quart baking dish with cooking spray, then spoon chicken mixture evenly into dish. Top with crushed potato chips, and bake at 350° for 25–30 minutes, or until bubbly.

Serve warm with crackers, rye toast points, or pita crisps.

Note:

To cook chicken: Place chicken in a medium saucepan with just enough water to cover and 1 teaspoon salt. Heat on medium heat until simmering; reduce heat to medium low, and cook, uncovered, 20 minutes or until cooked through. Remove from water, and rest 20 minutes before cutting.

Bacon-Wrapped Pineapple Jalapeño Poppers

When I was a little girl, I went to a wedding and had little finger sandwiches with some sort of pineapple cream cheese filling. I don't remember whose wedding it was, I don't remember if my dress was pretty, and I don't remember who caught the bouquet. What I did remember were those little sandwiches. (This is where Husband would jump in with a sarcastic, "You?") They had shredded green peppers and finely chopped bacon. Maybe minced onion? I dunno. But they were AH-MAZE-ING, and they left an impression. Obviously. So I decided to combine those ingredients with your basic popper recipe...and it turned out amazeballs! It's like the perfect storm in your mouth. You've got creamy cheese, sweet pineapple, spicy peppers, smoky bacon, and tangy barbeque sauce, all in one perfectly wrapped little package.

10 or more jalapeño peppers

1 (8-ounce) package cream cheese, softened

1 (20-ounce) can crushed pineapple in heavy syrup, drained well

1 (16-ounce) package bacon (not thick-sliced)

Barbeque sauce

Slice jalapeños lengthwise with a paring knife, then remove and discard the seeds and core. Do not do this with your bare hands; use latex gloves.

Beat cream cheese until fluffy. Add drained pineapple, and stir until thoroughly combined. Spread cream cheese mixture into jalapeño halves, leveling the top. You don't want to mound the cream cheese mixture into the jalapeños because the mixture will expand some when cooking.

Cut fatty ends off bacon (about 1½ inches total). Wrap each stuffed jalapeño with 1 slice bacon, and arrange on a large baking pan that's been sprayed lightly with cooking spray.

Bake poppers at 375° for 30–35 minutes or until bacon is crisp. Baste poppers with barbeque sauce, and continue baking for 5 minutes. Remove from oven and serve.

Makes 20 poppers.

Note:

This recipe makes enough filling for twice as many poppers. If you're making these for a party, double up on the peppers and bacon—trust me, you can't have too many of these! If not, refrigerate the leftover filling to use as a spread for bagels or crackers.

Bacon-Wrapped Pineapple Jalapeño Poppers

Party Shrimp

You're going to want to double or triple this recipe, because your party peeps are going to plow through them! You can cook these in minutes just as guests arrive.

1½ pounds large shrimp, peeled and deveined

1 package Italian dressing mix

¼ cup vegetable oil

½ teaspoon paprika

½ teaspoon garlic powder

¼ teaspoon cayenne pepper

Pinch of salt

Place shrimp in a large zip-top bag or lidded container. Whisk together dry dressing mix, oil, paprika, garlic powder, cayenne pepper, and salt until well combined; add to shrimp. Toss to coat shrimp, then refrigerate 1–4 hours.

Line a baking sheet with aluminum foil. Drain shrimp from marinade, then place shrimp in a single layer on baking sheet. (Discard marinade.) Broil shrimp on top rack of oven 5–7 minutes, or until pink and cooked through, flipping once during cooking.

Serve hot or at room temperature with cocktail sauce, if desired.

Makes 10–12 appetizer-size servings.

Bad Boys Stuffed Mushrooms

I made these bad boys on Christmas Eve, and they were AH-MAZE-ING! There's nothing to this. It's wicked easy and tastes divine! I think these will be hitting my tailgating menu and Super Bowl appetizer list. Fo sho!

2 (16-ounce) containers button mushrooms

1¼ pounds hot or mild Italian sausage (remove casings from sausage, if applicable)

1 (8-ounce) package cream cheese, softened

½ teaspoon garlic powder

1 tablespoon butter

Salt and pepper and taste

8 ounces mozzarella cheese, shredded (about 2 cups)

Chopped fresh chives or parsley for garnish (optional)

Note:

If you have any extra stuffing, spoon it into a small crock or ramekin, and heat while mushrooms are in oven. The stuffing is divine with crackers!

Prep mushrooms: Clean mushrooms by brushing away any dirt with a pastry brush or damp paper towel. Don't wash them, as they will absorb the water and not brown properly. Remove stems by applying pressure near where stem connects with cap. The stem will pop right off. If not, trim caps with a paring knife level with the gills. Chop stems.

Make stuffing: Cook sausage over medium heat in a large skillet until cooked through and crumbly. Remove sausage with a slotted spoon, and place in a large mixing bowl. Add cream cheese and garlic powder to sausage, and stir until well combined.

To sausage drippings, add butter, chopped mushrooms stems, salt and pepper, and sauté 5–6 minutes or until mushrooms are nicely browned. Add to sausage mixture, then add mozzarella, and stir to combine. Set aside.

Stuff mushrooms: Spray 2 cookie sheets with cooking spray, then arrange mushroom caps, gill-side up, on pans. Stuff each with stuffing mixture, mounding as high as you can (there's plenty). Bake, uncovered, at 375° for 20 minutes or until cheese is browned and bubbly.

Let stand 15 minutes before serving. Garnish with fresh chives or parsley, if desired.

Makes approximately 40 mushrooms.

Chipotle Shrimp Tostada Bites

Sometimes I look back on my adventure with Food Network, and I think "Did that really happen to me? Did I really get to be on America's Best Cook? Did I really ditch everything and fly up to New York to take my chances? Did I really get to work with chefs I've admired for years and years? Like Michael Symon and Alex Guarnaschelli and Cat Cora? I mean, come on?! Did that happen to me?"

There were hundreds of little moments emblazoned in my memory that I will cherish forever. What an amazing journey! Anywho, I'd been wanting to cook the shrimp I made for Cat again, so when I saw gulf shrimp at the market, I pounced on them. (And I didn't have to rip the heads off of these either, thankyouverymuch Food Network.) I whipped them up—as an appetizer this time—poured myself a beer, and let myself take a stroll back down memory lane.

Minus the marinade time, I can assure you this can be made in under 30 minutes, because I've done it. With 87 cameras in my face. And running for ingredients like a three-legged cat running for dirt.

1 (7-ounce) can chipotle peppers in adobo sauce

1 tablespoon minced garlic

¼ cup brown sugar

Juice of 1 lime

1½ pounds medium shrimp, peeled and deveined

1 (8-ounce) package prepared guacamole

1 bag bite-size round tortilla chips

Chopped cilantro

Finely diced red onion

Kosher salt

Combine chipotle peppers in sauce, garlic, brown sugar, and lime juice in a large bowl. Add shrimp, and stir gently. Cover and refrigerate 4–6 hours.

Cook shrimp on the grill, in a grill pan, or in a large skillet (grease with oil or cooking spray) over medium-high heat 2–3 minutes on each side or until shrimp are cooked through. Cook in batches so shrimp aren't overcrowded. Set aside.

To assemble, spread a dollop of guacamole onto each tortilla chip. Place 1 shrimp on top of each, then arrange tostadas on a serving platter. Sprinkle with cilantro, diced red onion, and salt. Serve within 1 hour of assembling.

Note:

Prepared guacamole is perfect for this! Easy, peesy, bo-deezy! I use Kroger's PeakFection.

Chipotle Shrimp Tostada Bites

Sriracha Bacon Deviled Eggs

So when we were invited to a friend's house to watch football games one Saturday, I was relieved to hear we would not be doing anything fancy, and that I could just bring a few pizzas for the kiddos. Roger that! But then I was feeling a little sketchy about not making something to take with me. I mean, that's what I do. I cook stuff.

I opened the refrigerator to find a whole lot of nothing staring back at me. I had bacon and eggs. That was about it. So I just decided to make deviled eggs. And then I got to thinking about adding the bacon to them. Which lead me to wonder what else I could add. Hot sauce. I like hot sauce on my scrambled eggs. Lots of it. Which leads me to Sriracha. Does anyone else like to imagine Scooby Doo saying 'Sriracha'? No? Moving on....

3–4 slices bacon

12 hard-boiled eggs, peeled

½ cup mayonnaise

2 tablespoons Sriracha sauce

¼ teaspoon salt

A good dash each of garlic powder, onion powder, and white pepper

Cook and crumble bacon. Make life easy and cook in the microwave, if you want.

Cut eggs in half lengthwise. Place yolks in a small mixing bowl, and arrange whites on a serving platter or plate.

To egg yolks, add mayonnaise, Sriracha, salt, and spices; mix well with an electric mixer or the back of a fork. If your filling is thick, add more mayonnaise, 1 tablespoon at a time, until you reach your desired consistency. Taste for salt and spices, and adjust.

Fill each egg white half with yolk filling (if you don't have a piping bag, this can very easily be done by using a zip-top bag with a small hole cut out of one corner). Top each egg with crumbled bacon. Cover, and refrigerate until ready to serve.

Makes 24.

Monte Cristo Party Sliders

You know those party rolls with ham and cheese that are baked with a buttery poppy seed topping? Well, I love them, and thought it would be fun to try a new take on those classic rolls. So I made a Monte Cristo version! When Husband saw me dusting them with powdered sugar, he was very disturbed, and thought I was ruining something that otherwise looked fantastic. I explained it was a classic flavor combination, but he still wasn't convinced and made me set aside a few without powdered sugar. But after he ate those, he grabbed one with the powdered sugar and loved it. Like, he really loved it. He even—y'all might want to sit down for this—told me he was wrong and I was right. He commented several times later in the day how that little bit of sweetness just "made" the rolls.

2 packs (12-count each) sweet dinner rolls (such as King's Hawaiian)

½ pound deli-sliced honey ham

½ pound deli-sliced smoked turkey

½ pound Gruyère, Emmental, or Muenster cheese, shredded or sliced

1 stick butter, melted

1 egg, well beaten

2 tablespoons Dijon mustard

Powdered sugar

Note:

To make an even more authentic Monte Cristo, consider serving with red currant jelly on the side.

Line a 9x13-inch baking pan with aluminum foil, and spray very lightly with cooking spray. (The foil makes it easy to remove from the pan.)

Remove rolls from packaging without separating them, and slice in half horizontally with a serrated knife (sort of making one giant rectangular hamburger bun). Place both bottom portions of rolls side-by-side in bottom of a baking pan.

Layer ham, turkey, and cheese evenly over rolls, then place top portion of rolls on top of cheese.

Whisk together butter, egg, and mustard; pour over tops of rolls, coating each one. Cover with tented foil (don't let foil touch rolls); bake at 350° for 20 minutes. Remove foil; continue baking 10 more minutes.

Remove from oven; let rest 15 minutes. Remove rolls from pan, and slice into single servings. When ready to serve, dust with powdered sugar (not before, as the powdered sugar will dissolve into the moisture on the rolls).

Blackberry Brie Tartlets

These little tartlets are super easy, affordable, and just beautiful to serve. This is definitely one of my go-to appetizer recipes. These can be changed up all sorts of ways to suit your taste (or what's in your fridge). I usually make several varieties. One eight-ounce wheel of brie makes exactly thirty tartlets...what you choose to jazz them up with is entirely up to you!

2 packages frozen mini phyllo pastry cups (30 total)

1 (8-ounce) round Brie

Blackberry jelly

OPTIONS:

Strawberry jam with thin jalapeño slices

Chutney

Apricot preserves

Candied ginger

Blue cheese crumbles with honey

Pepper jelly

Honey-soaked figs

Cranberry sauce and chopped walnuts

Pecan halves with honey

Note:

You can trim the rind off Brie or not...entirely up to you! I usually trim the top off and leave the rest.

Place phyllo cups on a baking sheet. Cut Brie into small pieces, and place in phyllo cups using all the cheese. Spoon a dollop of jelly (or other options) into each cup. Bake at 350° for 10–15 minutes, or until cheese is melted. Serve warm or at room temperature.

Variation:

Salted Pecan Brie Tartlets (pictured): Instead of jelly, place a pecan half in each cup on cheese, and sprinkle with salt. Bake as directed. Drizzle tarts with honey, then serve warm or at room temperature.

Bread & Breakfast

I've heard two theories as to where red-eye gravy got its name. The one I always reckoned was true when you serve it on grits, you make a little well or indentation in the grits to hold the gravy so it doesn't run all over the place and it kinda looks like a red eye.

The other I've heard is that when you add the coffee to the pan, the grease takes on a red tint and kinda swirls all together like a red eye. Since this makes me think of gasoline in a mud puddle and/or some creepy character in a sci-fi movie, I like to stick to the first theory.

Mama's Yeast Rolls

Thank goodness for Mama, because I am not a baker. I can just barely manage biscuits, but don't tell anybody that or I'll lose my street . It's always a special treat when Mama makes bread—especially rolls! I love to slather mine with good salted butter and strawberry preserves! They also make AH-MAZE-ING ham sandwiches!

4 teaspoons active dry yeast (a little less than 2 packets)

½ cup warm water

½ cup plus 1 teaspoon sugar

2 cups milk, at room temperature

7–8 cups all-purpose flour, divided

3 tablespoons butter, melted

2 eggs

2 teaspoons salt

Combine yeast, 1 teaspoon sugar, and warm water in a small bowl, and mix well. Let mixture rest about 5 minutes, or until yeast activates and mixture becomes foamy. Combine yeast mixture, ½ cup sugar, milk, and half of flour, then mix at medium speed for 2 minutes with an electric mixer or stand mixer fitted with a paddle attachment.

Add melted butter, eggs, and salt, and mix well. Begin mixing in remaining flour, 1 cup at a time, until dough pulls away from side of bowl. If using a stand mixer, switch to the dough hook attachment, and run on LOW 4 minutes. If making by hand, turn dough out onto a lightly floured surface, and knead 4 minutes.

Grease inside of a large mixing bowl, place dough in bowl, and turn over once to grease the top. Cover bowl with a clean kitchen towel, and allow to rise in a warm place about an hour, or until dough has doubled in size. Punch dough down, and turn out onto a lightly floured surface. Roll dough out until ½ inch thick, then cut into 2- to 3-inch squares; lightly shape into round rolls (just soften the corners so your rolls aren't square). Place rolls onto greased baking pans 2 inches apart. Cover pans with kitchen towels, and allow dough to rise again in a warm place about an hour, or until dough has doubled in size.

Bake rolls at 350° approximately 15 minutes or until golden brown.

Howdy Hoe Cakes

Vegetable oil or shortening

1⅓ cups self-rising cornmeal

⅔ cup self-rising flour

1 teaspoon sugar (optional)

¾ cup milk or buttermilk

¼ cup vegetable oil or melted bacon grease

2 eggs, beaten

Heat ¼ inch of oil in a large skillet over medium-high heat. While oil is heating, combine remaining ingredients, and mix until just combined.

Once skillet is good and hot, reduce heat a little, then pour batter into skillet like you're making 3–4 small pancakes.

Once bubbles appear throughout the batter, and edges are golden brown, flip and cook on other side until golden brown. Serve immediately.

Makes 8 servings.

Cream Biscuits

No need to cut the shortening or butter into the flour with cream biscuits! The cream is all you need, and these beauties come together so easily.

2¼ cups self-rising flour, plus more for dusting

1⅓ cups heavy cream

Melted butter

Combine flour and cream in a mixing bowl, and stir just until combined. Turn dough out onto a floured surface, and pat into a 1-inch thick slab with floured hands (add more flour, if dough is too tacky). Fold slab in half, then fold it again in the same fashion. Roll dough with a rolling pin until it is 1 inch thick.

Using a biscuit cutter or juice glass, cut dough into biscuits. Place biscuits onto a lightly greased baking pan 2 inches apart. Brush with melted butter, then bake at 475° for 10–12 minutes or until light brown on top.

Makes 8 servings.

"Cinnamon Roll" Biscuits

I love these! They have all the yummy goodness of an ooey, gooey cinnamon roll without all the work.

BISCUITS:

2 cups self-rising flour, plus
   more for dusting

½ cup powdered sugar

1 teaspoon cinnamon

½ cup shortening

½ cup milk

1 cup chopped pecans

GLAZE:

1 cup powdered sugar

Pinch of salt

¼ teaspoon vanilla extract

4–5 teaspoons milk

Add flour, powdered sugar, and cinnamon to a large bowl, then cut in shortening with a fork or pastry cutter until butter is pea-sized. Add milk and pecans, and stir just until dough comes together.

Turn dough out onto a floured surface, and pat into a 1-inch thick slab with floured hands (add more flour, if necessary, to keep the dough from being too tacky). Fold slab over like you're closing a book, then roll dough with a rolling pin until it is 1 inch thick.

Using a biscuit butter, empty can, or juice glass, cut dough into 8–9 Biscuits. Place Biscuits into a lightly greased round cake pan (Biscuits will touch). Bake at 450° for 12–14 minutes or until light brown on top.

While Biscuits are still hot, make the Glaze by stirring powdered sugar, salt, vanilla, and milk (start with 1 tablespoon, then add 1 teaspoon at a time) until smooth and spreadable. Spread Glaze over Biscuits, and serve immediately.

Makes 8–9 servings.

Blueberry Muffins with Lemon Glaze

I just love blueberries and lemon together! Not only are the blue and yellow gorgeous together, but the flavors complement each other so well!

MUFFINS:

1 cup blueberries

2 cups self-rising flour, divided

⅓ cup sugar

¾ cup milk

1 egg, beaten

¼ cup vegetable oil

GLAZE:

1 cup powdered sugar

1 tablespoon lemon juice

Zest of 1 lemon

Wash, then dry blueberries thoroughly with paper towels. Once dry, combine blueberries with ¼ cup flour, and gently toss to coat; set aside.

Combine remaining flour with sugar, milk, eggs, and oil, and mix until just combined.

Spray 12 muffin cups with cooking spray or line with paper baking cups. Divide batter evenly into cups, then bake at 400° for 15–17 minutes or until light golden brown.

Combine powdered sugar, lemon juice, and lemon zest (add more lemon juice, if necessary, to make the Glaze thin enough to spread). Spread over hot Muffins, and serve immediately.

Makes 12 servings.

Oh My Hash and Eggs

Oh my. That's about all I could manage to say when I took this out of the oven and looked at it. Oh. My. I don't think I've ever seen anything so pretty in all my life! I didn't even care if it tasted good at that point because it was so gorgeous! I mean look at it! Talk about starting your day off right! I was so full of it for the rest of the day, it didn't matter what came my way.

And the best part? It did taste good! It tasted AH-MAZE-ING, actually! The egg whites sort of hold onto some of the hash, so the servings lift out in these nice little bundles, and the yolks are rich and silky, and just coat everything perfectly!

And the other best part? It all cooks in one pan! I think this is the cleanest my kitchen's ever been after cooking a big Sunday breakfast. I made some toast (which totally goes perfectly with this), and I was done and done!

1 pound ground beef

1 large onion, diced

2–2½ cups diced potatoes (about 3 medium potatoes)

1½ teaspoons salt

1½ teaspoons pepper

1 teaspoon garlic powder

1 teaspoon Worcestershire

1 teaspoon paprika

1 teaspoon parsley (optional)

6 large eggs

Preheat oven to 350°. Heat a large cast-iron skillet (or other oven-safe skillet) over medium-high heat. Add ground beef, onion, potatoes, salt, and pepper, and cook, stirring frequently, until beef is no longer pink. Add garlic powder, Worcestershire, paprika, and parsley, and continue cooking until potatoes are tender.

Reduce heat to medium low. Using the back of a spoon, make 6 indentions in the hash. Don't go all the way to the bottom of the pan; just make a little well large enough to cradle the eggs. Break 1 egg into each indention. Season eggs with additional salt and pepper. Cook on stove until whites are mostly set and only partially translucent.

Carefully move skillet to oven, and bake 4–7 minutes or until whites are cooked through and yolks are cooked to preference. Serve with toast.

Makes 6 servings.

Oh My Hash and Eggs

Ham with Red-Eye Gravy

It just about don't get much more southern than red-eye gravy! I grew up eating it—mostly at Nanny's house. And since Nanny spent half her life in a dirt-floor house, I think it's safe to call this one old school. Fo sho.

For those of you who have never had red-eye gravy, I need to warn you—this isn't really gravy. It's more like a hot liquid that's only slightly reduced. It runs all over the plate and gets on everything. My favorite way to have this is with fried ham, fresh-sliced tomatoes, and biscuits. I end up mixing half my tomatoes into my grits and sop it all up with a biscuit. Man, dang! My mouth is watering.

1 pound thick country ham or cured ham slices (country ham is customary)

1 tablespoon bacon grease or vegetable oil

1 tablespoon butter

½ cup strong black coffee

½ cup water

Pinch of salt

Biscuits (about 6)

Heat a medium or large cast-iron frying pan over medium heat (you can use other types of frying pans, but the best red-eye gravy is made in a cast-iron skillet). Add bacon grease or vegetable oil to hot pan, then fry ham until nicely browned on each side. (Do not cook at a higher heat than medium—you do not want your pan drippings to burn or brown too much, or your gravy will taste burnt.)

Remove ham from pan, then add butter. Stir butter until melted, then add coffee. Using a wooden spoon, scrape up all the lovely ham bits from the pan. Add water and salt, then continue cooking over medium heat until the gravy is simmering. Once simmering, cook 4–5 minutes or until gravy is slightly reduced. Taste for salt and add, if necessary. Serve over ham and a biscuit.

Note:

We make our coffee really strong, so I usually make my red-eye gravy with half coffee and half water and let it reduce a little. If you make your coffee on the weak side, you can probably use all coffee, and omit the water.

Sausage Biscuit Breakfast Casserole

1 (16-ounce) can biscuits

1 pound breakfast sausage

6 eggs, beaten

1 cup milk

½ teaspoon salt

¼ teaspoon pepper

8 ounces Colby Jack cheese, shredded

Separate biscuits, and cut each into 8 pieces. Spray a 9x13-inch baking pan with cooking spray, then arrange biscuit pieces evenly in pan.

Cook and crumble sausage until cooked through; drain fat, then spread sausage over biscuit pieces.

Combine eggs, milk, salt, and pepper, and mix well. Pour egg mixture over sausage. Sprinkle cheese over top, and bake at 350° for 35–45 minutes or until cheese is light golden brown.

French Toast Bread Pudding

Making French toast for a crowd has never been so easy. Serve this with some bacon and sausage links, and you've got breakfast covered!

6 eggs, beaten

1¾ cups milk

1 cup cream

½ cup sugar

2 teaspoons vanilla extract

1 teaspoon cinnamon

¼ teaspoon salt

1 loaf French bread or brioche

½ stick butter

Powdered sugar

Combine eggs, milk, cream, sugar, vanilla, cinnamon, and salt in a large bowl, and mix well.

Cut bread into 1½-inch cubes; add to egg mixture, and gently fold to combine. Pour mixture into a greased 9x13-inch baking dish.

Cut butter into thin pats, and place evenly on top of bread mixture. Bake at 350° for 45–50 minutes or until golden brown.

Remove from oven, and let rest 10 minutes. Sprinkle with powdered sugar, and serve with syrup (just like French toast).

Makes 8 servings.

Breakfast Cake with Hot Maple Syrup

I love to make this when we have overnight guests. It's such a surprise to everyone! Most folks are a little stumped by it, but once they pour that hot syrup on and take a bite, they're hooked. You better be ready to write the recipe out, because everyone's going to ask you for it!

1 pound hot breakfast sausage

1 small onion, chopped

1 cup chopped red bell pepper

1 cup chopped green bell pepper

1 cup shredded Cheddar or Monterey Jack cheese

1 egg, beaten

½ teaspoon salt

½ teaspoon pepper

½ teaspoon garlic powder

2 cups biscuit mix

¾ cup milk

¼ cup sour cream

Real maple syrup, heated

Spray a 9x9-inch baking pan with cooking spray; set aside.

Cook and crumble sausage, onion, and peppers in a large skillet until sausage is cooked through; drain fat, and remove from heat.

Add cheese, egg, salt, pepper, and garlic powder to sausage mixture, and stir to combine; set aside.

Mix biscuit mix, milk, and sour cream in a large bowl. Add sausage mixture to dough mixture, and stir until all ingredients are evenly combined. Pour batter into prepared pan, and bake at 350° for 35–45 minutes or until golden brown. Cut into squares and drizzle with hot maple syrup to serve.

Makes 9 servings.

Breakfast Cake with Hot Maple Syrup

Spinach and Sausage Quiche

1 (10-ounce) box frozen
    chopped spinach, thawed

1 pound breakfast sausage

1 medium onion, diced

2 teaspoons minced garlic

8 ounces Swiss cheese,
    shredded (about 2 cups)

1 (9-inch) deep-dish pie pastry
    (optional)

4 eggs, beaten

1 cup milk

1 teaspoon salt

½ teaspoon pepper

Pinch of nutmeg

Drain spinach very well, then add to a large bowl; set aside.

Cook and crumble sausage in a large skillet over medium-high heat until sausage is cooked through. Remove sausage with a slotted spoon, and add to spinach. Add onion to sausage drippings, and sauté until translucent. Add garlic, and continue cooking 2 minutes. Add cooked onion mixture to spinach.

Add cheese to spinach mixture, and mix well. Pour spinach mixture into pie pastry, or a greased 9-inch deep-dish pie plate, if you make crustless.

Combine eggs, milk, salt, pepper, and nutmeg, and pour over spinach mixture.

Bake at 350° for 45–60 minutes or until golden brown and set in the center.

Makes 8 servings.

Soups, Stews & Chilis

Don't tell my husband this, but sometimes I don't mind those Sundays when I'm trapped at home with 47 loads of laundry to do. Those are the days I put a hearty soup on the stove, like this Buffalo Chicken Chili, and love on it all day while wearing yoga pants and a sweatshirt.

Do you love me less to imagine me with miss-matched socks and my hair yanked back with a headband? And a maternity sweatshirt that Husband has threatened to divorce me over if I ever try to wear it to Walmart again?

Ham and Beans

I think just about every part of the country has some dish made with ham (or perhaps sausage) and some sort of dried beans. Where I'm from, we usually like to use dried butter beans. I serve mine over white rice topped with diced onion, but you can also serve this as a hearty soup. Either way, you're going to want a big ole hunk of skillet cornbread to go with it!

1 pound dried small butter beans (baby lima beans)

1 ham bone with trimmings, or 2 ham hocks

5 cups water

1 teaspoon salt, plus more to taste

1 small onion, diced

½ teaspoon garlic powder

¼ teaspoon white pepper

Note:

I use white pepper in these to keep things light, but you can substitute ½ teaspoon black pepper.

Rinse beans per package instructions; add to a large pot or Dutch oven. Add remaining ingredients; cover, and heat over medium heat until boiling. Reduce heat to low, and simmer 3–4 hours or until beans are tender.

Remove ham bone from pot to cool. Add more salt, if needed. (I make mine a little on the salty side, since I serve them over plain white rice, so I usually have about 2 teaspoons total in mine.)

Once ham is cool enough to handle, remove meat from bone, then cut or shred into small pieces. Add ham pieces to beans; stir well before serving.

Makes 10–12 servings.

Southern-Style Vegetable Beef Soup

There's really no wrong way to make vegetable beef soup. If you don't like cabbage, leave it out. If you like barley, throw some in there! I find that many soups taste best when they've sat on the stove to rest a bit before serving, but I think it's especially true with vegetable beef soup!

2–3 tablespoons vegetable oil

2 pounds stew meat or chuck roast, cut into cubes

Salt and pepper to taste

1 cup chopped onion

1 cup chopped carrots

2 cups chopped cabbage

3 cloves garlic, minced

2 (32-ounce) cartons beef broth

1 cup lima beans or butter peas

1 cup sliced okra

1 cup fresh or frozen corn

1 (28-ounce) can petite diced tomatoes, undrained

1 (14-ounce) can cut green beans, undrained

½ teaspoon thyme

½ teaspoon Italian seasoning

Put enough oil in a soup pot to coat bottom, and heat over medium-high heat. Season beef with salt and pepper, then sear in hot pot, working in batches, if necessary. Remove beef from pot, and set aside.

Add onion, carrots, cabbage, and garlic to pot; sauté for 5 minutes. Add beef broth and remaining ingredients, and stir well. Add water to pot, if necessary, so that all ingredients are covered with liquid. Bring mixture to a slow boil. Add salt and pepper to taste, cover, reduce heat, and simmer for 1 hour.

Makes 10–12 servings.

Bean and Bacon Cheeseburger Soup

What I love about this soup is that it's super hearty. I always found regular bean and bacon soup to be a little puny on its own. I want some MEAT in my soup. This has all the smoky goodness of traditional bean and bacon soup with chunks of ground beef and gobs of creamy cheese. It is so good!

1 pound dried Great Northern or navy beans

6 cups vegetable or chicken broth

2 cups water

1 pound lean ground beef

1 onion, diced

Black pepper and garlic powder to taste

12 slices thick-cut bacon

1 teaspoon salt (plus more to taste)

1 tablespoon Worcestershire

⅔ cup half-and-half

2 cups shredded Colby cheese, divided

Combine beans, broth, and water in a Dutch oven or large pot. Cook, covered, over medium-low heat 2 hours.

In a large skillet, sprinkle ground beef and onion liberally with black pepper and garlic powder; cook over high heat until beef is cooked through and seared nicely. Add to bean pot along with any drippings. Don't drain. (As long as you use lean ground beef and cook at a high temperature, there shouldn't be an excessive amount of pan drippings.)

Cut bacon into small pieces; cook until crispy in a large skillet. Drain on paper towels, then add bacon to pot, reserving about a cup for garnish, if desired.

Add salt, Worcestershire, and additional pepper and garlic powder to taste; stir well. Cover, and cook 1–2 hours until beans are very tender.

Add half-and-half and 1½ cups shredded cheese to pot; stir well. Serve with remaining ½ cup cheese and reserved bacon pieces, if desired.

Makes 10–12 servings.

Italian Lentil Soup with Sausage

When I visited QVC to sell my first cookbook, I decided to take Mama with me. I figured it would be a fun way for us to spend some time together. I was right! (Side note about that—David Venable is a riot, and QVC is a class-act all the way. I am a forever-fan of both!)

We spent some time in Philadelphia and discovered Reading Terminal Market downtown. It's an indoor market filled with food venders (think food trucks meet farmers market) with every cuisine and culture you can imagine—and then some.

One dish that really made an impression on me was a bowl of spicy sausage and lentil soup. I'm not even sure if I'd ever even eaten lentils before, but one spoonful of that soup, and I was hooked! I came home, picked up some lentils at the store, and immediately got to cooking my own version. Just as delicious as the vendor's!

1½ pounds Italian sausage, casings removed, if applicable

2 tablespoons olive oil

2 cups diced onions

1½ cups diced carrots

1½ cups diced celery

3–4 cloves garlic, diced

6 cups chicken broth

2 cups water

1 (15½-ounce) bag garlic and herb lentils

Brown and crumble sausage over medium to medium-high heat in a Dutch oven or large pot until cooked through (take care not to scorch or burn). Using a slotted spoon, remove sausage from pot; set aside.

Add olive oil, onions, carrots, and celery to pot; sauté until onions become translucent, 4–5 minutes. Add garlic, and continue cooking 2 minutes.

Add broth, water, lentils with seasonings from included packet, and sausage to pot; bring to a boil. Reduce heat to medium low, cover, and cook 40 minutes, or until lentils are tender. Turn off heat and let rest, covered, 20 minutes before serving.

Makes 8–10 servings.

Creamy Chicken and Potato Soup

This reminds me so much of chicken pot pie! The soup has a rich stock with chicken and potatoes that finishes with a little cream at the end for the perfect amount of richness, without being too heavy. The chicken sort of poaches in the stock, so you don't have to cook it separately. If you'd like yours creamier, use a cup less broth and add one additional cup of half-and-half.

1 medium onion, diced

3–5 celery stalks, diced (about 2 cups)

2–4 carrots, diced (about 2 cups)

⅓ cup (5 tablespoons) butter

⅓ cup all-purpose flour

1 (32-ounce) carton chicken broth

1½ teaspoons salt (plus more to taste)

1 teaspoon pepper

1 teaspoon thyme

1 teaspoon garlic powder

3–4 medium potatoes, peeled and diced ¾ inch

3 chicken breasts

1 cup half-and-half

Sauté onion, celery, and carrots in butter in a Dutch oven or soup pot until onion becomes translucent, about 5 minutes. Add flour; cook and stir 2 minutes.

Add broth, salt, pepper, thyme, and garlic powder; stir until well combined and smooth. Once simmering, reduce heat to medium low, then add potatoes and chicken breasts. Cover, and cook 30 minutes, stirring occasionally.

Remove chicken to a cutting board or plate. Cover loosely, and allow chicken to cool. Uncover pot, increase heat to medium, and allow soup to continue cooking 30 additional minutes. (This way we can reduce the stock a bit for better flavor without overcooking the chicken, and when we're ready for it, the chicken will have properly rested, so it will be juicy and tender.)

Taste soup, and add more salt (or the other spices), if desired. Reduce heat to low.

Cut chicken into small pieces; add to soup along with half-and-half. Stir to combine, then cover and continue cooking 10–20 minutes on low.

Makes 8–10 servings.

Creamy Chicken and Potato Soup

Potato Chowder with Sausage and Kale

This chowder reminds me very much of Olive Garden's Zuppa Toscana Soup. I make it like a thick and hearty potato soup, but add lots of garlic and Italian sausage and a little kale at the end. The sausage gives the chowder just the right amount of heat, and then the kale gets just a little wilted, but still has a slight bite. Perfection!

1¼ pounds hot Italian sausage, casings removed, if applicable

1 onion, diced

6 cloves garlic, minced

4 cups chicken broth

5–6 medium yellow potatoes

Salt to taste (about a teaspoon)

1 pint half-and-half

1 bunch fresh kale, chopped (approximately 4 cups)

Brown and crumble sausage over medium-high heat in a Dutch oven or soup pot until no longer pink. Add onion and garlic; continue to cook 2–3 minutes. Add chicken broth.

Wash potatoes, and cut into ¼-inch slices. (I don't peel mine, but you can if that's your preference.) Add potatoes to pot, and salt to taste. Bring broth to a low boil, cover pot, reduce heat to medium low, and continue cooking 40 minutes.

While whisking rapidly, slowly pour in half-and-half. Continue whisking until smooth and creamy. (This is necessary to emulsify fat from sausage into broth and cream, and it also helps to break up potatoes into rustic chunks.) Taste for seasoning. Continue cooking until chowder just begins to simmer, 10–15 minutes.

Remove from heat, stir in kale, cover, and let stand 10 minutes before serving.

Makes 8–10 servings.

Guinness Stew

I usually lean toward a big ole skillet of cornbread with soups and stews, but this Guinness Stew is glorious served with big slices of crusty sourdough bread slathered with butter. The alcohol cooks out of the beer, so don't let that scare you off. You'll love how rich and hearty this stew is!

2–3 tablespoons vegetable oil

2 pounds boneless chuck roast, trimmed, cut into 1-inch cubes, seasoned with salt and pepper to taste

½ cup all-purpose flour

2 large onions, chopped

3–4 cloves garlic, minced

1 tablespoon tomato paste

4 cups beef broth

1 (11.2-ounce) bottle Guinness Stout beer

1 teaspoon salt

½ teaspoon black pepper

1½ cups chopped carrots

1½ cups chopped celery

2 cups coarsely chopped, peeled potatoes

Put enough oil in a Dutch oven or large pot to coat bottom; heat over medium-high heat. Dredge seasoned beef in flour. Sear half the beef on all sides, then remove from pan. Repeat with remaining beef.

Add onions and garlic to pot; cook 4–5 minutes, stirring occasionally. Stir in tomato paste; cook 1 minute. Stir in broth and beer, scraping pan to loosen up any browned bits. Add beef back to pot, then stir in salt and pepper. Bring pot to a slow boil, then reduce heat to low, and simmer, covered, for 1 hour or until meat is tender.

Add carrots, celery, and potatoes, and return to a slow boil. Simmer stew, uncovered, 45 minutes or until potatoes are very tender. Thicken with a little cornstarch mixed with water, if desired.

Makes 8–10 servings.

Country Beef Stew

Using short ribs in stew adds some extra flavor and helps thicken it. You can substitute ox tails, shanks, or any other bone-in cuts for the ribs.

4 tablespoons olive oil, divided

1½–2 pounds chuck roast, cubed (or stew meat)

1–1½ pounds beef short ribs

Salt, pepper, and garlic powder to taste

2–3 cups diced carrots

2–3 cups diced celery

1 large onion, diced

5–6 cloves garlic, minced

½ teaspoon thyme

¼ cup all-purpose flour

2 envelopes beefy onion soup mix (such as Lipton's)

4½ cups water

1 cup dry red wine

2 tablespoons Worcestershire

1 bay leaf

4–5 medium potatoes, peeled and cubed

Heat 3 tablespoons olive oil in a Dutch oven or large pot over medium-high heat. Season meat and ribs liberally with salt, pepper, and garlic powder. Add meat and ribs in batches to hot oil, and brown on all sides. Remove with a slotted spoon; set aside. We're not looking to cook the meat through at this point.

Add remaining 1 tablespoon oil, carrots, celery, and onion to pot; sauté 4–6 minutes until onion is translucent. Add garlic and thyme; cook 2–3 minutes. Add flour, and stir well. Cook and stir 2–3 minutes.

Combine soup mix with water; stir into veggies until smooth and well combined; stir in wine and Worcestershire. Add meat and ribs with any juices back to pot. Add bay leaf and potatoes; stir well. Reduce heat to low, cover, and slowly simmer 3–4 hours, stirring occasionally. Do not let it boil!

When ready to serve, remove rib bones and bay leaf from pot.

Makes 8–10 servings.

Notes:

I really don't think there's a substitute for the wine, but if you absolutely must, use beef broth plus one additional tablespoon Worcestershire.

Country Beef Stew

Son-Of-A-Gun Oyster Stew

The last time we had oysters, Daddy said, "You know, the first fella to crack open an oyster, see what it looked like on the inside, and decide to eat it anyway must have been one hungry son of a gun." And isn't that the truth?! But I'm so glad someone discovered how delicious they are, because I sure do love them! You can buy shucked oysters at the coast in any of the dockside markets (and those are insanely delicious!), but the ones sold near the seafood department in your grocery store will work just fine.

1 large onion, diced

1 cup diced celery

2 cloves garlic, minced

1 stick butter

¼ cup all-purpose flour

1 quart shucked oysters (about 4 dozen), liquid reserved

3 cups whole milk

1 cup half-and-half

1 large bay leaf

Salt and pepper to taste

Tabasco sauce

Oyster crackers

Sauté onion, celery, and garlic in butter until onion is translucent. Add flour; continue cooking for 2 minutes while continuously stirring. Add reserved oyster liquid, milk, half-and-half, and bay leaf. Add salt and pepper to taste. Bring mixture to a slight boil; reduce heat to low and simmer, uncovered, 30 minutes.

Add oysters, and cook 3–4 minutes until oysters begin to curl.

Serve with a few shots of Tabasco and oyster crackers.

Makes 8–10 servings.

Honky Tonk Cabbage Stew

Many, many, many moons ago, I worked as a cook at a little honky tonk out in the country. We mostly just served stuff like burgers and chicken wings. Except on Wednesdays. On Wednesdays, we cooked a big homemade meal. One Wednesday I arrived at work to find Ms. Sandy (a Michigan transplant who'd recently moved to town) in the kitchen. The first thing I thought was, "Who let this Yankee in my kitchen?!" She was cooking a ham bone with cabbage and potatoes. Well, that seemed like a great start to me, but when she dumped a couple cans of cream of whatever soup in there, I thought she'd lost her mind. Well, guess what? It was really good. Years later, I thought about that cabbage stew, and made my own version—and it is now officially one of my favorite stews!

1 pound smoked sausage or kielbasa, cut into bite-sized pieces

2 tablespoons vegetable oil

1 onion, chopped

1–2 carrots, grated

3–4 tablespoons bacon grease (can substitute butter)

1 small head cabbage, chopped into 1-inch pieces

1 teaspoon salt

½ teaspoon pepper

¼ teaspoon garlic powder

6 cups chicken broth

5 medium potatoes, peeled and cubed

1 (10¾-ounce) can cream of celery soup

Sauté sausage in vegetable oil in a large stockpot or Dutch oven until nicely browned. Add onion and carrots, and continue cooking until onion is semi-translucent. Add bacon grease, cabbage, salt, pepper, and garlic powder; continue cooking and stirring for 5 minutes.

Add chicken broth and potatoes; mix well. Reduce heat to medium-low; cover, and simmer 30 minutes, or until potatoes are tender.

Stir in cream of celery soup, reduce heat to low, cover, and continue cooking 10–15 minutes. (As always, I think all soups and stews are BEST if you turn off the heat and let them sit about 30 minutes or until they're just above room temperature, but I understand if you can't wait!)

Makes 8–10 servings.

Catfish Stew

Mama and Daddy go fishing. A lot. Their freezer is always stocked with local freshwater goodness like bream, crappie, rock fish (striped bass), and catfish. Yay for me, because Husband doesn't much care for any of it (eating it or fishing for it), so I can always get my fix at their house. When I'm itching for some Catfish Stew, I can always hit up their freezer for just what I need!

5 strips thick-cut bacon or fatback, cut into ½-inch pieces

1 medium onion, diced

½ cup diced celery

1 (14-ounce) can petite diced tomatoes, undrained

1½ cups water or fish stock

3 tablespoons ketchup

1 tablespoon Worcestershire

1 teaspoon salt

½ teaspoon black pepper

½ teaspoon thyme

½ teaspoon red pepper flakes

3 medium potatoes, peeled and diced

1 pound catfish fillets, cut into 1-inch pieces

Brown bacon or fatback in a Dutch oven or soup pot over medium-high heat until almost crisp. Add onion and celery; sauté until tender.

Add tomatoes, fish stock, ketchup, Worcestershire, seasonings, and potatoes; stir well. Reduce heat to medium low, cover, and cook 40 minutes, or until potatoes are very tender.

Add catfish, reduce heat to low, cover, and continue cooking 10 minutes. Remove from heat, stir, cover, and rest 20 minutes before serving.

Makes 4–6 servings.

Tip:

You might be lucky enough to find canned fish or seafood stock in your grocery store. If you do, you won't need a full teaspoon of salt for this recipe. Just salt to taste.

Chili Mac

I make my Chili Mac much like I make chili, then I just add macaroni noodles, milk, and cheese to turn it into one big hearty pot of goodness we can usually stretch into two suppers. This is great for feeding a crowd on a cold winter day. Kids love it, it's inexpensive to make, and it will warm you up from the inside!

1½ pounds ground beef

1 onion, diced

Salt, pepper, and garlic powder to taste

1 (15-ounce) can chili beans, undrained

1 (14-ounce) can petite diced tomatoes

1 (8-ounce) can tomato sauce

1 packet chili seasoning

1 teaspoon salt

½ teaspoon pepper

½ teaspoon garlic powder

½ teaspoon cumin

1 cup milk

1½ cups small macaroni noodles, uncooked

2 cups shredded Cheddar or Colby Jack cheese, divided

Season ground beef and onion with salt, pepper, and garlic powder; brown in a Dutch oven or soup pot until meat is cooked through. Drain fat, if desired.

Add remaining ingredients, except 1 cup cheese. Stir well, cover, and bring to a boil. Reduce heat to low; cook, covered, 15 minutes, stirring occasionally. Turn off heat and let pot rest, covered, for 15 minutes, or until liquid is absorbed and noodles are tender. Stir again, then top with remaining shredded cheese to serve.

Makes 10–12 servings.

Note:

Chili beans are pinto beans with chili seasoning. If you can't find chili beans, just use a can of your favorite beans.

Buffalo Chicken Chili

As soon as the temperatures drop in the fall, I'm always itching to make a big ole pot of something that requires a spoon to eat! Something piping hot!

2 pounds chicken breasts (3–4 breasts)

1 (1-ounce) packet dry ranch dressing mix

1 cup diced onion

1 cup diced celery

½ cup diced carrots (optional)

⅔ stick butter

5–6 cloves garlic, minced

6 cups chicken broth

1–2 cups water

1 pound dried Great Northern or navy beans

1 teaspoon salt

½ cup hot wing sauce (or more to taste)

Crumbled blue cheese and diced green onions for garnish (optional)

Wash chicken breasts, and place in a medium bowl. Coat thoroughly with dry ranch dressing mix (I use my hands). Cover, and refrigerate to marinate until ready to use (overnight is better).

In a Dutch oven or large pot, sauté onion, celery, and carrots in butter 3–4 minutes. Add garlic, and continue cooking 2 minutes. Add broth, 1 cup water, beans, and salt; stir well, and bring to a boil. Reduce heat to low, cover, and cook beans at a slow simmer 2 hours. Check beans throughout cooking, and add more water, if needed. It is necessary to maintain enough liquid for beans to cook, but not so much that things become soupy (you want to maintain a "chili-like" consistency).

After 2 hours, add chicken, cover, and continue cooking over low heat 2 more hours.

Remove chicken from pot, and cover tightly with aluminum foil; set aside. Continue cooking beans for 1 more hour or until tender.

Cut cooled chicken into bite-sized pieces. Add to beans with hot wing sauce; stir well. Remove from heat and let rest, covered, 15–20 minutes.

Serve with blue cheese crumbles and diced green onions, if desired.

Makes 8–10 servings.

Buffalo Chicken Chili

Slow Cooker Chicken Chili

The first time I made this chili, I didn't think it would ever make it to the table, because the entire state of South Carolina went under water. An overabundance of rain from Hurricane Joaquin hit us hard in 2015, and wreaked havoc on my beloved state. Roads washed out, bridges collapsed, dams burst, power was lost, and most were without water for weeks.

Just as the chili was finishing up, we lost power. I was anticipating this, and had already pulled my car up by the back door. I've got one of those nifty vehicles with standard plug-ins in the back for tailgating, so I was fully prepared to tote my slow cooker out to the car and finish cooking this glorious chili in the flood. Thankfully, the beans were cooked through, so I didn't have to battle the flood to finish supper... but I was prepared to!

3 large bone-in, skin-on chicken breasts, or 1 whole chicken

Salt and pepper to taste

1 pound dried pinto beans

1 packet chili seasoning mix

4 cups chicken broth

2 (14-ounce) cans petite diced tomatoes, undrained

1 large onion, diced

1 jalapeño pepper, seeded and diced

5–6 cloves garlic, minced

½ teaspoon salt

½ teaspoon cumin

½ teaspoon chili powder

Cilantro (optional)

Season chicken breasts with salt and pepper; set aside. In a large slow cooker, put beans, chili seasoning, broth, tomatoes, onion, jalapeño, garlic, salt, cumin, and chili powder; mix well.

Place chicken on top of chili mixture. Cover; cook on HIGH 5–6 hours until chicken is cooked through.

Remove chicken, and wrap tightly with aluminum foil. Taste beans, and add more salt (and/or other seasonings from the recipe), if desired. Reduce heat to LOW, and continue cooking 2 hours, or until beans are tender.

Remove and discard skin and bones from chicken; shred with a fork, or cut into cubes. Add chicken to chili, mix well, then turn off heat; let rest, covered, for 45 minutes to 1 hour (this will thicken the chili).

Serve with fresh cilantro, if desired.

Makes 10–12 servings.

Salads

Since we live slap in the middle of South Carolina, we like to take off for the beach or the mountains for the weekend. I always make chicken salad, ham salad, pimento cheese, tuna salad, and/or my Easy Peasy Egg Salad to take with us on road trips or make while on vacation. We might go out to eat for supper now and then when we're on vacation, but for the most part, we eat in. Especially for lunch. They make THE best sandwiches and don't require me to drag out 47 different condiments and 18 packs of lunch meat and cheese. All you need is bread. Easy peasy!

Dawn's Delicious Grape Salad

I'd never had or heard of grape salad, so when my dear friend, Dawn, showed up with it at Thanksgiving, I was seriously scratching my head. And I was secretly wondering if this was some crazy Ohio thing, since that's where she's from. I immediately fell in love with it after one bite! This is her exact recipe, and I've never changed a thing. It's perfect!

2 pounds green seedless grapes

2 pounds red seedless grapes

1 (8-ounce) package cream cheese, softened

1 cup sour cream

½ cup sugar

1 teaspoon vanilla extract

1½ cups brown sugar

1½ cups chopped nuts

Wash grapes, and pluck off stems. Dry grapes completely. (I usually do this by setting them out on clean kitchen towels for a few hours.)

Combine cream cheese, sour cream, sugar, and vanilla; mix until smooth.

In a large bowl, gently fold cream cheese mixture with grapes until all grapes are coated. Spoon into a large bowl or baking dish (anything big enough to hold everything).

Combine brown sugar and chopped nuts; mix well. Sprinkle brown sugar and nuts evenly over grape mixture. Refrigerate until ready to serve.

Makes 14–16 servings.

Best Fresh Fruit Salad Ever!

This recipe happened by pure-T accident. I love to keep fresh fruit around the house, especially in the summer when it's all so good. I like to wash and chop it, then throw it in a plastic container for easy snacking.

So one day...I'd cut up some strawberries in a bowl. Then I noticed I had one single lonely green apple. Well, he needed to be with those strawberries. And so did that handful of grapes, and half a pineapple.

I tossed it all together, and realized I'd need to do something to the apple, or it would turn brown. So I squeezed the juice of a lemon all over everything. And that made it all sour. So I added sugar to it. And y'all. Y'ALL! The lemon juice and sugar made this sort of glaze that coated everything, and it was glorious!

1 pint strawberries, halved or quartered

½ pineapple, chunked

1 mango, peeled and chopped

1 green apple, chopped

2–3 cups red seedless grapes

2 bananas, peeled and sliced

Juice of 1 lemon

¼ cup sugar

Put all fruit into a large bowl. Combine lemon juice and sugar, and stir well (sugar won't dissolve immediately, but it will after a few minutes). Pour over fruit. Serve, or cover and refrigerate to store.

Makes 8–10 servings.

Note:
If you halve the grapes, they are easier to eat with a fork.

Crunchy Oriental Ramen Salad

Remember this salad?! When I was growing up, I used to get soooo excited when Mama would make this salad, because, A) it was so delicious, but most importantly because, B) I totally thought it was something special and exotic!

There are 40'leven different versions of this salad floating around out there, but this has always been my favorite.

1 (16-ounce) bag shredded coleslaw mix

1 cup diced snow peas or shelled edamame

1 cup diced scallions

1 (15-ounce) can Mandarin oranges, drained

1 cup sliced or slivered almonds

¾ cup vegetable oil

⅓ cup white vinegar

½ cup sugar

2 packs oriental-flavored ramen noodles

Combine coleslaw mix, snow peas (or edamame), scallions, Mandarin oranges, and almonds in a large bowl; set aside.

In a separate bowl, combine vegetable oil, vinegar, and sugar; whisk vigorously until well combined.

Open ramen packages and remove seasoning packets. Add contents of seasoning packets to the oil mixture, and whisk until well combined. Cover dressing, and refrigerate.

Just before serving, crumble ramen noodles over salad, then toss all with dressing.

Makes 8–10 servings.

Crunchy Oriental Ramen Salad

Mediterranean Orzo Salad

Maybe I like this recipe so much because orzo looks a lot like rice, and rice is my favorite food on the planet. Or maybe it's because it's delicious, travels well, and everyone loves it! This is great to take to potlucks and picnics, because there's nothing in it that will spoil if not refrigerated after a few hours. And it's just so different that everyone wants to try some! Don't skip the parsley; it really brightens up the salad!

16 ounces orzo pasta

1 English cucumber, diced

1 pint grape tomatoes, halved

1 red onion, diced

1 cup kalamata olives, pitted and halved

1 cup Greek salad dressing

1 cup crumbled feta cheese

½ cup chopped fresh parsley

Pepperoncini peppers for garnish

Cook pasta in liberally salted water per manufacturer's instructions for al dente preparation. Rinse in cold water, then drain thoroughly.

Combine cooked pasta with cucumber, tomatoes, onion, olives, and salad dressing; stir until well combined. Fold in feta cheese and parsley, then spoon into a serving bowl. Garnish the edges of the salad with pepperoncini peppers. Refrigerate until ready to serve. Feel free to add more Greek dressing, if desired.

Makes 14–16 servings.

Summer Corn Chopped Salad

I love adding fresh corn to salsa, quesadillas, and salads! All you have to do is toss it in the microwave for a few minutes for tender, crisp corn! The husks peel away, taking the silk with it. Boom! Done.

When you serve a salad like this, the greens are under all the chopped vegetables. So when folks serve themselves, they just scoop out what they want with a pair of tongs, and leave the things they don't. If someone doesn't like onions, they just steer clear of the mound of onions and so on and so forth. Everybody's happy!

2 ears fresh corn with husks

2 hearts of romaine lettuce, chopped

1 small red onion, chopped

1 orange bell pepper, chopped

1 pint grape tomatoes, halved

½ English cucumber, chopped

6–7 green onions, chopped

8–10 pieces bacon, chopped, cooked until crisp

Dressings of choice

Place both ears of corn in microwave, and heat on HIGH for 3 minutes. Remove from microwave, and cut stalk end off each ear. Peel husk and silks away. Slice kernels off each ear; set aside to cool.

Arrange romaine in bottom of a large, shallow serving bowl. Top romaine with piles of remaining vegetables and bacon. Cover and refrigerate until ready to serve.

To serve, provide tongs and 2–3 dressings for variety. I like to serve green goddess, ranch, and a vinaigrette.

Makes 8–10 servings.

Pizza Pasta Salad

I love to make pasta salads to keep on hand during the summer for quick lunches, and to have as side dishes to sandwiches. I especially like any pasta salad that isn't mayonnaise based, so I don't have to fret over keeping it ice-cold in case I want to bring some to the park or on a picnic.

What's great about this pasta salad is that the kids always scarf it down, because it tastes so much like pizza! Feel free to add more of your favorite pizza toppings!

12 ounces rotini pasta

1 pint grape tomatoes, halved

1 bunch green onions, chopped

1 green bell pepper, diced

1 (3.8-ounce) can sliced black olives, drained well

8 ounces mozzarella pearls

2 cups mini pepperoni slices

1 teaspoon dried oregano

⅓ cup freshly grated Parmesan cheese

¾–1 cup zesty Italian salad dressing (to taste)

Cook pasta in liberally salted water per manufacturer's instructions for al dente preparation. Rinse in cold water, then drain thoroughly.

Combine pasta with remaining ingredients, and toss to combine. Refrigerate in an airtight container.

Makes 10–12 servings.

Note:

Mozzarella pearls are small little balls of fresh mozzarella and can usually be found in the deli section. If you can't find them, substitute with diced fresh mozzarella.

Tuna Noodle Salad

As I've mentioned before, I'm old enough that when I was in college, people actually ate in the dorm cafeteria. So, whenever you or your roommate(s) went home for the weekend or a holiday, you always brought back food from home so you could skip the cafeteria food for a day or two. One of my favorite things that Shelly (my roomy and BFF) would bring back from home was a GIGANTIC Tupperware container of tuna noodle salad. I know—it doesn't sound like anything spectacular, but y'all, to this day it's one of my favorite comfort foods.

Sometimes I make it with chicken instead of tuna. Sometimes I add chopped boiled eggs. Sometimes I add diced celery or relish. You can make it any way you prefer! This is just a good base recipe to help you get started!

1 pound elbow macaroni noodles

2 (12-ounce) cans tuna, drained well

1½ cups mayonnaise

1 medium onion, diced

Salt and pepper to taste

Old Bay Seasoning (optional)

Cook pasta in liberally salted water per manufacturer's instructions for al dente preparation. Drain, then rinse in cold water. Drain again very thoroughly.

Combine noodles, tuna, mayonnaise, onion, and seasonings to taste; stir well. Refrigerate in an airtight container up to 1 week.

Makes 8–10 servings.

Note:

If you don't have Old Bay, that's okay. I use it because I think Old Bay just goes with anything at all to do with fish or shellfish, but also because it has a hefty amount of celery seed in it, which I think is perfect in any sort of mayonnaise-based salad.

Simple Seafood Salad

I never have understood why imitation crab got such a bad rep. It's not crab...right? Got that. But that doesn't mean it's not yummy. It's made out of fish. Granted, they process it and then shape it into the little pieces, but that's no different from how lunchmeat is made. When was the last time you saw a square ham or round turkey breast? Same deal, Lucille.

I love to make this to have with crackers, serve on a nice crusty roll, or to stuff pita with. If you're in the habit of making tuna salad for lunches and the like, try this as an alternative. I've yet to serve it to guests who didn't gobble it all up.

14 ounces imitation crab

½ cup mayonnaise

1–2 stalks celery (amount per preference), finely chopped

½ teaspoon Old Bay Seasoning

½ teaspoon dillweed

Salt to taste

Separate crab into individual pieces (only if compressed in package; if not, disregard), and chop into ½-inch pieces; add to a medium bowl. Add remaining ingredients, and gently stir until well combined. Serve immediately, or cover and refrigerate to store.

Makes 4–6 servings.

Note:

If you don't have any Old Bay, try Cavender's Greek Seasoning, or use a combination of celery salt and paprika.

Simple Seafood Salad

Easy Peasy Egg Salad

12 hard-boiled eggs, peeled and diced

⅔ cup mayonnaise

1 teaspoon mustard (yellow or Dijon)

¼ teaspoon salt

A dash each: onion powder, garlic powder, and white pepper

Chopped chives or green onions for garnish (optional)

Note:

I'm telling you not to add all the mayonnaise mixture at first, because you can't work backwards if you get it too soupy. If your eggs were smaller than mine, or your measurements weren't exact, or whatever, you might not need as much mayonnaise as I did, and I'd hate for you to have a runny batch of egg salad. Ya dig?

Add eggs to a large bowl; set aside.

In a separate bowl, combine mayonnaise, mustard, salt, onion powder, garlic powder, and white pepper; mix well.

Add most of the mayonnaise mixture to the boiled eggs (all but about 3 tablespoons). Stir well, then add remaining mayonnaise mixture to eggs, if desired. Add more salt to taste, if desired.

Garnish with chives or green onions, if desired.

Makes 8–10 servings.

Vegetables & Sides

"Southern-style" just means we cook vegetables low and slow until they're tender and delicious. And adding some bacon just brings it all together. I could make a meal out of a pot of green beans and potatoes like these...especially with a big ole hunk of cornbread to go with it!

Quick and Easy Asparagus

This asparagus only takes a few minutes to prepare. If you have any left over, chop and add to pasta salad, rice dishes, omelets, stir-fry, and fried rice!

2–3 cloves garlic

2 teaspoons olive oil

1 bunch fresh asparagus, fibrous ends removed

Coarse grain salt to taste

Peel garlic and smash with a chef's knife or spatula so that the cloves burst open, but remain mostly intact. Heat olive oil and garlic in a medium skillet over medium heat until garlic is fragrant and just starting to brown, 2–3 minutes. Remove garlic from oil. Remove garlic; discard.

Add asparagus and salt to oil, and sauté 3–4 minutes or until tender-crisp. Serve immediately.

Makes 3–4 servings.

Easy Slow Cooker Broccoli Rice Casserole

2 (10.75-ounce) cans cream of broccoli soup

1 (8-ounce) jar Cheez Whiz

¼ teaspoon garlic powder

1 (2-pound) bag frozen chopped broccoli

1 small onion, diced

1 cup Minute rice, uncooked

1 cup shredded Cheddar cheese

Combine soups (unprepared), cheese spread, and garlic powder in a large bowl, and mix well. Add broccoli, onion, and rice, and stir to combine.

Lightly spray a medium slow cooker with cooking spray, then spoon broccoli mixture into slow cooker. Cover and cook on HIGH 4 hours. Top with shredded cheese, cover, and continue cooking until cheese is melted.

Makes 6–8 servings.

Southern Fried Cabbage

This "frying" method is really just sautéing it in a little fat, then covering it with a lid so the water that's released from the cabbage can steam it. This is also exactly how I cook collard greens (and mustard or turnip greens). I love to serve this cabbage with smoked sausage and boiled potatoes for a quick supper!

1 head cabbage

3–4 tablespoons bacon grease or vegetable oil

Salt and pepper to taste

¼ cup chicken broth or water (if needed)

Cut cabbage into quarters, and remove core from each section. Chop cabbage into 1-inch pieces, and set aside. Heat bacon grease in large skillet over medium-high heat. Add cabbage, and toss to coat. Add salt and pepper to taste. Sauté cabbage about 10 minutes.

At this point, your cabbage should start releasing some of its water. If it doesn't, and your pan is mostly dry, add chicken broth or water, and toss to coat. Cover skillet, reduce heat to medium low, and continue cooking cabbage, stirring occasionally, approximately 30 minutes, or to your liking (I like mine a tad al dente).

Makes 6–8 servings.

Garlic Roasted Brussels Sprouts

Oven-roasting Brussels sprouts totally transforms them into something special. A lot of the moisture evaporates in the hot oven, so the flavors really get concentrated. The outside gets browned and caramelized, while the inside stays moist and tender! These are also amazeballs served with freshly grated Parmesan.

1½ pounds fresh Brussels sprouts

3 tablespoons olive oil, plus more for serving

1 teaspoon sea salt, plus more for serving

3–4 cloves garlic, minced, or 1 teaspoon garlic powder

Grated Parmesan (optional)

Tips for avoiding bitter sprouts:

• Smaller, heavier Brussels sprouts are less bitter.

• Cut large ones in half. This releases an acidic compound that can make larger Brussels sprouts taste bitter.

• Trim away as much of the stem as possible and any outside leaves that aren't tightly closed.

• Like greens, Brussels sprouts are best during the cold weather months.

Wash and dry Brussels sprouts, then add to a bowl. Cut any that are larger than an inch in diameter in half, keeping the small tender ones whole. Toss Brussels sprouts with olive oil, salt, and garlic; arrange in a single layer in a large baking pan (large enough to ensure the Brussels sprouts aren't touching and have plenty of room).

Bake at 400° for 18–20 minutes. Watch closely! You want a nice roasted char on the bottom, but there's a fine line between charred and burned.

To serve, spoon into a serving bowl; drizzle with additional olive oil, sprinkle with more sea salt, and top with Parmesan cheese, if desired.

Makes 6–8 servings.

Corn Casserole with Cheese and Bacon

I love that the corn is the star of this dish (sometimes it can get lost in a casserole). The contrasts in flavor and texture are perfect. The salty, smoky bacon balances the sweetness and the gooey, cheesy filling is perfect with the crispness of the corn.

2 eggs

2 tablespoons butter, melted

¼ cup all-purpose flour

2 tablespoons sugar

¼ teaspoon cayenne pepper

2 (12-ounce) bags frozen steam-in-the-bag corn, thawed (or 4½ cups fresh), divided

8 ounces Cheddar cheese, shredded (about 2 cups), divided

4 pieces bacon, cooked and crumbled (about ½ cup)

2 tablespoons chopped chives

Add eggs, melted butter, flour, sugar, cayenne, and 2 cups corn to a blender or food processor, and pulse 3–4 times to mix well and cream the corn.

Pour mixture into a medium bowl. Add remaining corn, ¾ of the cheese, bacon, and chives; stir to combine. Pour mixture into a greased 2-quart shallow baking dish, then sprinkle with remaining ½ cup cheese.

Bake, uncovered, at 325° for 30–35 minutes or until golden brown and bubbly around edges.

Makes 6–8 servings.

Fried Zucchini Sticks

I love, love, love to make this when we have Italian food, because I think it goes perfectly with it. Sometimes I skip the pasta altogether, and just serve the zucchini (the kids don't even notice!). I also really like to dip these in marinara sauce! SO GOOD! They taste a lot like mozzarella sticks, but they're better for you!

1 cup grated Asiago cheese (can substitute Parmesan)

1 cup Italian bread crumbs

1 teaspoon coarse grain salt, plus additional for finishing

2–3 whole zucchini

2 tablespoons cornstarch

2 eggs, well beaten

Vegetable oil

Combine grated cheese, bread crumbs, and salt in a shallow bowl; mix well. Set aside.

Wash zucchini; dry well. Cut ends off zucchini; cut each in half or thirds, depending on how long it is (you want sections that are about 3 inches long). Cut each section lengthwise into 8 sticks.

Add zucchini and cornstarch to a zip-top bag; seal, then shake to coat. (You can also do this in a lidded plastic bowl.) Place coated zucchini on a plate, shaking off excess cornstarch.

Dip each zucchini stick in beaten eggs; shake off excess. Dredge each in bread crumb mixture, taking care to thoroughly coat zucchini; shake off excess.

Add 1 inch of vegetable oil to a medium or large pot. Heat oil over medium heat until temperature reaches 325°. Fry slowly, so zucchini has time to get tender without the cheese burning. Fry until golden brown.

Cook in batches so as not to overcrowd pan. Sprinkle with additional salt right when you remove zucchini sticks from hot oil. Serve with marinara sauce or as is.

Makes 6–8 servings.

Fried Zucchini Sticks

Southern-Style Baked Beans

You know how you lay slices of bacon on top of baked beans so you get that glorious smokey flavor? Except that the bacon shrinks up so much during cooking that only the center of your dish has bacon, and it's impossible to cut them with the serving spoon, so only five people actually get the bacon? Yep, you know.

Here's my solution to the bacon dilemma! I top my favorite baked beans with a gazillion nuggets of bacon that crisp up and work their magic while the beans are cooking. End result? Bacon for everyone!

½ cup ketchup

½ cup barbeque sauce

¼ cup brown sugar

1 tablespoon yellow mustard

1 tablespoon Worcestershire

A few drops liquid smoke (optional)

¼ teaspoon garlic powder

¼ teaspoon pepper

2 (28-ounce) cans basic pork n' beans, drained

5–6 slices thick-cut bacon

Combine ketchup, barbeque sauce, brown sugar, mustard, Worcestershire, liquid smoke, garlic powder, and pepper in a medium-size bowl, and mix well; set aside.

Add beans to ketchup mixture. Mix gently with ketchup mixture until thoroughly combined. Pour into a shallow 2-quart baking dish.

Cut bacon into ½-inch pieces; place pieces evenly in a single layer on top of beans. Bake beans, uncovered, at 350° for 1 hour, or until bacon is cooked through and starting to crisp.

Makes 12–14 servings.

Note:

Don't use any beans labeled "baked beans" or "barbeque beans" or anything fancy like that, as they're already jazzed up. You just want plain-Jane, inexpensive pork n' beans for this recipe.

Southern-Style Green Beans and Potatoes

2 pounds fresh green beans

8 slices bacon

1 onion, diced

3–4 large Yukon Gold potatoes, peeled

4 cups chicken broth

3 tablespoons butter

1 teaspoon salt

1 teaspoon pepper

Note:

Sometimes I like to use whole small red potatoes (we call them "new" potatoes). You can use just about any type of potato—except baking potatoes—they won't hold up being boiled this long.

Wash and trim beans; cut into 2-inch pieces, and set aside.

Cut bacon into ½-inch pieces; sauté over medium heat in a large skillet until browned. Add onion and beans; continue to sauté until onion is translucent. Remove from heat.

Cut potatoes into large cubes, and add to a large pot or Dutch oven. Add chicken broth, butter, salt, pepper, and bean mixture (with pan drippings) to the pot; bring to a boil. Cover, reduce heat to medium low, and cook 30–45 minutes, stirring occasionally. Let rest 10 minutes before serving.

Makes 6–8 servings.

Twice-Baked Potato Casserole

This is such a great recipe for special occasions. It can sit a while, until everything else is ready, without losing any of its creamy deliciousness. All the toppings you could ever want on a baked potato are already in the dish, which makes it very easy to serve.

5 pounds baking potatoes, peeled

1 (8-ounce) package cream cheese, softened

1 stick butter, softened

1 cup sour cream

¼–½ cup milk

⅓ cup chopped fresh chives

8 ounces Cheddar cheese, shredded (about 2 cups), divided

1 teaspoon salt

½ teaspoon garlic powder

½ teaspoon pepper

Paprika for garnish

Cut potatoes into 1-inch cubes. Boil in salted water for 20 minutes, or until tender. Drain well.

Combine boiled potatoes, cream cheese, butter, and sour cream in a large mixing bowl, and mix on low speed with an electric mixer. Add ¼ cup milk, and continue mixing until smooth, adding more milk, if needed.

Stir in chives, half the cheese, salt, garlic powder, and pepper, and stir until well combined. Evenly spoon mixture into a greased 3-quart baking dish. Top with remaining cheese, and sprinkle with paprika.

Bake at 350° until cheese is golden brown and bubbly.

Makes 10–12 servings.

Greek Potatoes

I'm not a fan of overly tart Greek potatoes (seriously…some of them are just too pucker-inducing), so I don't use a ton of lemon juice. I do like the flavor, so I use the zest, too. This gives you all those yummy lemony notes without an overpowering amount of sourness.

I also like to use both olive oil and butter. I love the traditional Greek flavor from the olive oil, and the creaminess from the butter.

4–5 pounds small to medium russet potatoes

1 lemon, juice and zest

¼ cup olive oil

¼ cup butter, melted

1½ teaspoons salt

1 teaspoon oregano

1 teaspoon garlic powder

½ teaspoon pepper

½ teaspoon paprika, plus more for dusting

1½ cups chicken broth

¼ cup chopped fresh parsley (optional)

Wash and peel potatoes. Cut in half lengthwise, and place in large bowl. Pour lemon juice over potatoes. Add olive oil, butter, salt, oregano, garlic powder, pepper, and paprika to potatoes; mix well.

Place potatoes in a single layer in a 9x13-inch baking pan. Slowly pour broth into pan, taking care not to pour broth over potatoes (we don't want to rinse off any seasonings). Dust potatoes with a little additional paprika.

Cover pan tightly with aluminum foil; bake at 375° for 40 minutes. Remove foil, and continue baking potatoes 30–40 minutes or until just tender. Remove potatoes from oven, cover again with foil, and let rest for 15 minutes before serving.

Remove foil, then sprinkle potatoes with reserved lemon zest and parsley, if desired.

Makes 8–10 servings.

Notes:

• The parsley is optional, but I think it's worth the spend.

• Definitely let the potatoes rest before serving to soak up all of those yummy pan juices!

Southern Cornbread Dressing with Sausage

My family's favorite dish at Thanksgiving isn't the turkey. It's the cornbread dressing! When I want to make it extra special, I add sausage to my dressing.

1 family-size pan cornbread (enough to serve 10–12)

1 pound ground sausage

1 onion, diced

3–4 celery stalks, diced (about 2 cups)

½ cup butter

2 cups chicken or turkey broth

1 (10.75-ounce) can cream of chicken soup

½ teaspoon salt

½ teaspoon poultry seasoning (or more to taste)

Crumble cornbread into small pieces into a large mixing bowl; set aside.

Cook and crumble sausage in pan until cooked through and nicely browned. Drain fat, then add to the bowl of cornbread (do not stir yet).

Sauté onion and celery in butter 4–5 minutes, or until onion is semi-translucent. Add veggies and butter to the bowl of cornbread (do not stir yet).

Combine chicken broth, cream of chicken soup, salt, and poultry seasoning in a mixing bowl; whisk together until smooth. Pour into bowl with cornbread mixture, and gently fold to combine.

Spoon mixture into greased 9x13-inch baking dish. Bake, uncovered, at 350° for 25–35 minutes, or until lightly browned and heated through.

Makes 10–12 servings.

Notes:

- Do not use a sweet cornbread recipe when making dressing.

- If you prefer a more dense and loaf-like dressing, stir ingredients really well before spooning into the dish.

- My family also really likes to add chopped boiled eggs! I think that's a regional thing.

Chicken and Dressing Casserole

If you're itching for a taste of Thanksgiving, but don't want to cook for three days to get it, try this casserole! This is also great to take to a holiday dinner, because it has so many of the traditional T-Day trimmings all in one yummy dish.

3 chicken breasts

1 (14-ounce) can chicken broth

3 stalks celery, finely diced

1 small onion, finely diced

6 tablespoons butter

1 (10.75-ounce) can cream of chicken soup

1 teaspoon salt

½ teaspoon poultry seasoning, or more to taste

½ teaspoon pepper

¼ teaspoon garlic powder

1 (8-inch) pan cornbread, crumbled

3 hard-boiled eggs, peeled and diced (optional)

Slowly cook chicken breasts in broth over medium-low heat in a covered pot until cooked through. Remove chicken, and allow to cool, then shred with 2 forks, or dice into bite-sized pieces; cover and set aside. Measure out 2 cups of chicken stock, and set aside.

Meanwhile, sauté celery and onion in butter until onion is translucent.

Combine reserved 2 cups chicken stock, cream of chicken soup, salt, poultry seasoning, pepper, and garlic powder, and stir well.

In a large mixing bowl, combine cornbread, chicken, sautéed veggies (with butter), chicken stock mixture, and eggs, if desired; mix well. Spoon mixture into a greased baking dish and cook, uncovered, at 350° for 45 minutes or until nicely browned on top.

Makes 6–8 servings.

Southern-Style Slow Cooker Macaroni and Cheese

One year, Mama called me the week before Thanksgiving and said she wanted us to try a slow cooker mac and cheese recipe to free up some real estate in the oven. I wasn't thrilled at the thought. I mean, you just can't go screwing around with something as important as macaroni and cheese on Thanksgiving! But I tend to do what my mama says. So I had to figure this thing out.

Our traditional baked mac and cheese uses eggs to help it set up. The edges get all golden brown and crusty, and the center stays soft and melty. How to get all that from a slow cooker? On any normal day, I wouldn't fret, and just hope it turned out edible. But this was Thanksgiving! I was still having reservations about trying something new on The Big Day, but I went for it. And it was a total hit! It cooked up almost exactly like my baked mac and cheese and tasted perfect!

12 ounces (2 heaping cups) uncooked elbow macaroni

1 (12-ounce) can evaporated milk

1½ cups milk

½ cup sour cream

2 eggs, beaten

1 teaspoon salt

½ teaspoon dry mustard

½ teaspoon white pepper

¼ teaspoon cayenne pepper

4 tablespoons butter, melted

16 ounces Cheddar cheese, shredded, divided (4 cups)

Boil macaroni in liberally salted water for 5 minutes, then drain well. Do not cook noodles longer than 5 minutes.

While noodles are cooking, combine evaporated milk, milk, sour cream, eggs, salt, mustard, white pepper, and cayenne pepper in a large bowl, and mix well.

Add parboiled macaroni, melted butter, and 3 cups shredded cheese to milk mixture, and stir until thoroughly combined.

Spray the inside of a medium-large slow cooker (approximately 4-quart size) with cooking spray, then pour macaroni mixture in. Top with remaining 1 cup cheese. Cover and cook on LOW for 3–4 hours, or until set in center and golden brown around edges.

Makes 10–12 servings.

Southern-Style Slow Cooker Macaroni and Cheese

Sausage and Rice Casserole

This simple dish made with sausage and rice is perfect for supper, side dishes, potlucks, and Thanksgiving (sometimes called Rice Dressing or Rice Stuffing). Consider making two at a time, because the leftovers heat up beautifully!

1 pound pork sausage

1 medium onion, diced

1½ cups finely diced celery

¼ teaspoon red pepper flakes (optional)

1 (14-ounce) can chicken or vegetable broth (about 1¾ cups)

1 (10.75-ounce) can cream of celery soup

1 cup uncooked white rice

Brown and crumble sausage in a large skillet. When sausage is about half cooked, add onion, celery, and red pepper flakes, and continue cooking until sausage is no longer pink, and veggies are starting to become translucent. If your sausage is particularly fatty, drain some of the fat.

In a bowl, whisk together broth and soup until smooth. Pour soup mixture and rice into skillet, and stir until all ingredients are thoroughly incorporated.

Pour into a buttered 2-quart casserole dish, cover tightly with aluminum foil, and bake at 350° for 1 hour. Remove casserole from oven, and let rest, covered, for 10–15 minutes before serving.

Makes 3–4 entrée servings, or 6–8 side-dish servings.

Chicken & Seafood

We eat a LOT of chicken and rice dishes at my house. There's chicken pilaf, dirty rice, jambalaya, and more that we just don't even have names for. But the one dish that everyone asks for by name is Chicken Bog. Chicken Bog isn't just food; it's an event! You don't just cook a little bit of Chicken Bog. You cook a washtub full of it, then invite a crowd over to help you eat it.

Sticky Chicken

Nanny used to make something we called Sticky Chicken. The skin would be sticky, and the meat would just fall off the bone. Nanny's chicken always had a red glazed look to it, and a touch of sweetness, too. Since she never wrote down her recipe for it, I had to use my best judgement as to what all was in it. Think I got it!

8–10 bone-in, skin-on chicken thighs and/or legs

⅓ cup honey

¼ cup ketchup

2 tablespoons soy sauce

2 tablespoons hot sauce

1 tablespoon Worcestershire

1 tablespoon minced garlic

Place chicken in a large zip-top bag or resealable container. Combine remaining ingredients, and pour over chicken. Marinate in refrigerator 6–10 hours (or overnight).

Add just enough oil to a large cast-iron skillet to coat bottom. Heat (see below for alternate preparation also) over medium heat. Once hot, add chicken pieces, reserving marinade. (The honey in the marinade can burn on high heat, so be sure to have your temperature at medium—hot enough to bubble and sizzle, but not hot enough to scorch the chicken.) Cook chicken on all sides just until browned. (We're not trying to cook the chicken through.)

Pour marinade over chicken in skillet. Place uncovered in oven; bake at 325° for 1 hour, basting chicken 3–4 times during the hour.

Makes 6–8 servings.

Alternate Preparation:

If you don't have a cast-iron skillet or a frying pan big enough to fit all the chicken pieces, don't worry! Just brown the chicken in batches in any sturdy skillet. Transfer browned chicken to a 9x13-inch baking dish, pour reserved marinade over chicken, and bake and baste per recipe.

Firecracker Chicken

This is like Chinese take-out that you can make at home. Despite the name, the dish isn't overly spicy (feel free to add more red pepper if you want to kick up the heat!). I think one of my favorite things about this recipe is that it finishes in the oven, which gives you time to get everything else ready for supper and on the table.

Vegetable or canola oil

4 large boneless, skinless chicken breasts

Salt, pepper, and garlic powder to taste

1 cup cornstarch

4 eggs, beaten

½ teaspoon salt

SAUCE:

½ cup hot sauce

1¼ cups brown sugar

2 teaspoons soy sauce

¼ teaspoon garlic powder

¼ teaspoon red pepper flakes

Heat ½ inch oil in a large skillet over medium-high heat.

Cut chicken into 1½-inch pieces; season liberally with salt, pepper, and garlic powder. Coat chicken with cornstarch; set aside.

Beat eggs with ½ teaspoon salt, then quickly dip cornstarch-coated chicken pieces in eggs, shake off excess, and fry in hot oil on both sides until light golden brown. Cook in batches to ensure you don't overcrowd pan.

Place browned chicken pieces in a very large baking dish (you don't want to have more than 2 layers of chicken in the pan, or it will get soggy); set aside while you make the Sauce.

Whisk together Sauce ingredients until smooth. Pour over chicken, then gently stir to coat. Bake, uncovered, at 325° for 45 minutes, stirring once after 25 minutes.

Serve with white rice and steamed vegetables, if desired.

Makes 6–8 servings.

Buttermilk Ranch Roasted Chicken with Potatoes

Of all the recipes I've created in my day, I think I'm most proud of this one. This is a true one-pan wonder of juicy, tender chicken that cooks up with perfectly roasted, delicious potatoes you'll be proud to serve.

2 tablespoons olive oil

1 teaspoon salt

1 teaspoon garlic powder

1 teaspoon onion powder

½ teaspoon white pepper

½ teaspoon black pepper

10 pieces bone-in, skin-on chicken thighs and/or legs

3 pounds small red potatoes, rinsed and cut in half, if necessary (you don't want any bigger than 2 inches in diameter)

1½ cups buttermilk ranch dressing (not the mix)

Coarse-grain salt

Chopped fresh parsley (optional)

Note:
Check the ingredients list on the dressing to be sure buttermilk is one of the top three ingredients. Do not buy light or fat-free dressing.

Combine olive oil, salt, garlic powder, onion powder, and white and black peppers in a large shallow bowl. Add chicken, and massage spices into chicken.

Coat 2 (9x13-inch) baking pans with cooking spray. Arrange chicken pieces evenly in pans; bake at 325° for 45 minutes.

Place potatoes cut-side down in pans, arranging evenly around chicken. Return to oven; continue cooking 30 minutes.

Baste chicken and potatoes with dressing. Sprinkle potatoes with a little coarse-grain salt. Don't flip or turn them. Return to oven; continue cooking 30 minutes.

Baste chicken and potatoes with dressing again. Increase oven temperature to 375°; continue cooking 20–30 minutes, or until chicken is golden brown.

Serve on a platter garnished with chopped fresh parsley, if desired.

Makes 6–8 servings.

Buttermilk Ranch Roasted Chicken with Potatoes

All-Star Chicken with Cajun White Barbeque Sauce

This is my new favorite thing to make at cookouts! We grill up the chicken, then serve it on buttered buns with Cajun White Barbeque Sauce. It's a great alternative to grilling burgers if you have a crowd to feed. I like a few slices of dill pickle on the bottom, too. It all comes together pretty easily, and you can serve this chicken on its own or as a sandwich—either way, it's an all-star recipe!

12–14 boneless, skinless chicken thighs

½ cup soy sauce

½ cup Worcestershire

½ cup Dijon mustard

¼ cup brown sugar

3 tablespoons vegetable oil

½ teaspoon garlic powder (or more to taste)

1 teaspoon black pepper

½ teaspoon salt

CAJUN WHITE BARBEQUE SAUCE:

1½ cups mayonnaise

3 tablespoons apple cider vinegar

1 tablespoon Dijon mustard

1 teaspoon Cajun seasoning

½ teaspoon black pepper

Trim any excess fat from chicken, then place in a gallon zip-top bag or lidded container. Make a marinade by combine soy sauce, Worcestershire, mustard, brown sugar, oil, garlic powder, pepper and salt. Pour over chicken. Seal bag, and refrigerate 6–8 hours or overnight.

Drain marinade, and discard. Grill chicken over medium heat 15–20 minutes, or until cooked through.

Serve as is, or on buns with Cajun White Barbeque Sauce.

CAJUN WHITE BARBEQUE SAUCE:

Combine all ingredients; refrigerate until ready to serve. Use as a condiment, fry sauce, or basting sauce.

Note:

I really prefer using thighs over breasts, because you just about can't overcook them. They stay moist and juicy and have so much more flavor!

Southern Country-Fried Chicken with Milk Gravy

You can use this same method for traditional Southern-style fried chicken using bone-in, skin-on pieces, and increasing the temperature of the oil to 350 degrees.

3–4 large fresh boneless, skinless chicken breasts, cut into 2 cutlets and pounded flat

1–2 cups buttermilk

Salt and pepper to taste

2 eggs

¼ cup hot sauce

2 cups all-purpose flour

2 teaspoons salt

1 teaspoon pepper

1 teaspoon paprika

1 teaspoon thyme

1 teaspoon garlic powder

1 teaspoon white pepper

½ teaspoon cayenne pepper (optional)

MILK GRAVY:

¼ cup pan drippings

¼ cup reserved flour mixture

3 cups milk

Salt to taste

Place chicken in a plastic zip-top bag or lidded container; add buttermilk to coat. Seal bag, and marinate 4–6 hours (or overnight). Drain chicken; lightly season with salt and pepper; set aside.

Whisk together eggs and hot sauce in a shallow bowl; set aside.

Combine flour and remaining ingredients in a large bowl; mix well. Reserve ¼ cup mixture for gravy; set aside.

In a large pan or skillet, heat 3–4 inches of oil or shortening to 325°. Dredge each piece of chicken in flour, and shake off any excess. Dip in egg wash; shake off excess. Dredge in flour once more, to thoroughly coat; shake off excess.

Fry chicken in hot oil until dark golden brown on the outside and juices run clear. Cook in batches so not to overcrowd pan. Serve with gravy.

Makes 6–8 servings.

MILK GRAVY:

Pour off all but ¼ cup of pan drippings. Whisk in flour mixture, and cook over medium heat 2–3 minutes until light brown. Slowly whisk in milk. Cook and whisk until gravy is thick and smooth. Add salt to taste.

Chicken Parmesan

I have had a lot of experience making this recipe, because it's my husband's all-time favorite. Any time I ask him what he wants for supper, he wants Chicken Parmesan.

This is my absolute favorite way to prepare and serve it. You can cook the pasta and heat the sauce while the chicken is getting happy in the oven, and everything's ready to serve at once. Plus when you let the chicken bake in a little bit of sauce, it gets even more tender and juicy!

3 large boneless, skinless chicken breasts

Salt, pepper, and garlic powder to taste

2 eggs

2 tablespoons water

¾ cup Italian bread crumbs

¾ cup freshly grated Parmesan cheese, plus more for garnish

1 teaspoon garlic powder

½ teaspoon salt

Vegetable oil

1 (24-ounce) jar marinara sauce

8 ounces mozzarella, shredded (about 2 cups)

12 ounces spaghetti or linguine

Chopped fresh parsley (optional)

Cut each breast into 2 cutlets (reducing the thickness by half). Gently pound out with a meat mallet until flattened. Season both sides with salt, pepper, and garlic powder. Set aside.

In medium bowl, whisk eggs and water; set aside.

Combine bread crumbs, Parmesan cheese, garlic powder, and salt in a shallow bowl; set aside.

Heat ¼ inch oil in a large skillet over medium to medium-high heat. (Oil should be hot enough to fry, but not to burn the Parmesan cheese.)

Dip each cutlet in egg wash, and shake off any excess. Dredge in bread crumb mixture; shake off excess. Fry chicken on both sides in hot oil until golden brown. Cook in batches, so not to overcrowd the pan. Drain on paper towels.

Pour half the marinara sauce in bottom of a 9x13-inch baking pan; arrange chicken in a single layer over sauce. Top with mozzarella; bake at 350° for 20–25 minutes or until cheese is melted.

Heat remaining marinara. Cook pasta in liberally salted water per package instructions.

Serve chicken with pasta and sauce. Garnish with freshly grated Parmesan and parsley, if desired.

Makes 4–6 servings.

Chicken Parmesan

Chicken Cacciatore

I get really excited about putting something like this on the table! The chicken stews in the tomato sauce and literally falls off the bone. It's a perfect Sunday dinner, because you can throw it in the oven and forget about it for awhile.

I like to serve this family style by removing the chicken from the pan, stirring the pasta into the sauce, then replacing the chicken atop the pasta in the pan.

8–10 pieces bone-in, skin-on chicken thighs and legs

Salt and pepper to taste

Olive oil

1 green bell pepper, sliced

1 large onion, sliced

5–6 cloves garlic, minced

½ cup red wine

1 (28-ounce) can crushed tomatoes, undrained

2–3 teaspoons sugar

2 teaspoons Italian seasoning

2 teaspoons oregano

½ teaspoon red pepper flakes

1 pound angel hair pasta

Parmesan cheese

Fresh basil (optional)

Season chicken pieces liberally with salt and pepper. Add enough oil to a large skillet to coat bottom; heat over medium-high heat. (Do NOT use a cast-iron skillet as it will react to red wine and tomatoes.) Once oil is hot, add chicken, and brown on all sides. Cook in batches, so not to overcrowd the pan. Set browned chicken aside.

Add green pepper and onion to pan; sauté 3–4 minutes. Add garlic; continue cooking 2 minutes. Add red wine to deglaze pan; cook 7–8 minutes, or until wine is reduced by half.

Add tomatoes, sugar, and seasonings; stir well. Cook until bubbly, then remove from heat. Taste; add more salt and pepper, if desired. Pour sauce into a baking dish; add chicken, cover with aluminum foil, and bake at 350° for 1½ hours. Remove foil, baste chicken with sauce, and continue cooking 10 minutes, or until skin has absorbed sauce.

Let dish rest, uncovered, 15 minutes.

Meanwhile, cook pasta in liberally salted water per package instructions. Serve pasta with sauce and chicken pieces.

Makes 6–8 servings.

Slow Cooked Smothered Chicken with Mushroom Gravy

I don't cook with mushrooms much, because I'm the only one at my house who likes them. What's great about this recipe is that you can easily pluck the mushrooms out of the gravy if someone you're serving doesn't like them.

3–4 large boneless, skinless chicken breasts

Salt, pepper, and garlic powder to taste

Olive oil

8 ounces crimini (baby bella) or button mushrooms, sliced

¼ teaspoon thyme

½ stick butter

⅓ cup all-purpose flour

2 cups chicken broth

Cut each chicken breast into 2 thin cutlets (reducing the thickness in half, not the width). Season both sides of each cutlet with salt, pepper, and garlic powder; set aside.

Pour just enough olive oil into a large skillet to coat bottom; heat over medium-high heat. Once pan is hot, brown chicken pieces on each side, then set aside. (We're not cooking them through, just searing them on each side.) Work in batches, so not to overcrowd the pan.

Once all chicken pieces are browned and removed from pan, reduce heat to medium; add mushrooms, thyme, and butter to pan; season with a little pepper, and sauté 3–4 minutes.

Add flour to pan; stir to coat. Continue cooking 2 minutes. Slowly add chicken broth. Stir and cook about 5 minutes, or until gravy is thickened and smooth. Add more salt, if necessary.

Add chicken cutlets to slow cooker; cover with mushroom gravy. Cook on LOW 4 hours or HIGH 2 hours. (You can also return cutlets to gravy in the pan, cover, and cook on low for 1 hour.)

Serve with egg noodles, mashed potatoes, or rice.

Makes 4–6 servings.

Chicken Lazone

Chicken Lazone is a dish that originated in New Orleans from Brennan's restaurant. My version is super simple to make, and always a show-stopper. The chicken sizzles in butter until golden brown and delicious! Be prepared to see grown people licking their plates when you make this, because the sauce is irresistible!

2 teaspoons garlic powder

1 teaspoon onion powder

1 teaspoon chili powder

1 teaspoon paprika

½ teaspoon white pepper

1 teaspoon salt

2 pounds chicken breast tenderloins

1 stick butter, divided

3 cups real, heavy cream

10–12 ounces spaghetti, cooked

Combine garlic powder, onion powder, chili powder, paprika, white pepper, and salt in a small bowl. Reserve 1½ teaspoons spice mixture. Season chicken with remaining spice mixture.

Heat 3 tablespoons butter in a large skillet over medium heat until sizzling. (Don't get butter too hot, or it will burn.) Add half the chicken pieces; cook until nicely browned. Add 1 more tablespoon butter; flip chicken, and brown on the other side. Once chicken is nicely browned on both sides, remove from pan. Repeat this process with remaining chicken pieces and butter.

Slowly add cream and reserved 1½ teaspoons spice mixture to drippings in skillet; heat over medium heat until simmering, stirring slowly. Once simmering, continue to cook over medium heat 10–15 minutes, or until thick and creamy. Add additional salt and/or garlic powder to taste.

Serve chicken and sauce over cooked spaghetti.

Makes 6–8 servings.

Cajun Chicken Lasagna

My kiddos don't even care that there are chopped vegetables in this dish, because it's all swimming in Alfredo sauce. They'd eat a two-by-four if I slathered it with Alfredo sauce! Laissez les bon temps rouler, y'all!

- **1 pound andouille sausage, diced**
- **3 large boneless, skinless chicken breasts, cut into bite-sized pieces**
- **1–1½ teaspoons Cajun seasoning**
- **1 bell pepper (any color), diced**
- **1 large onion, diced**
- **3 stalks celery, diced**
- **3–4 garlic cloves, minced**
- **2 (15-ounce) jars prepared Alfredo sauce**
- **9–12 lasagna noodles, cooked**
- **2 cups shredded mozzarella cheese**

Note:
Andouille is a cured Cajun link sausage. If you can't find it in your area, substitute with smoked sausage or chorizo.

Brown andouille in a large skillet over medium-high heat. Remove sausage; set aside.

Season chicken with 1 teaspoon Cajun seasoning, then add to hot skillet with pan drippings. Sauté chicken until just done, adding a little vegetable oil, if necessary, to prevent sticking. Remove chicken; set aside.

Add bell pepper, onion, celery, garlic, and a dash of Cajun seasoning to drippings in skillet. Sauté until tender and fragrant. Remove from heat, and stir in 1 jar Alfredo sauce. Add more Cajun seasoning, if desired; set aside.

Coat a 9x13-inch baking dish with cooking spray. Arrange 3–4 lasagna noodles on bottom (whatever fits your dish). Arrange half the sausage and half the chicken on top. Spoon half the Alfredo vegetable mixture over meat. Sprinkle half the mozzarella over vegetable mixture. Repeat layers; top with remaining 3–4 lasagna noodles.

Pour remaining jar of Alfredo sauce over top. Tent with foil (to prevent it from resting on sauce), and bake at 350° for 1 hour. Remove from oven, and rest, covered, 15–20 minutes before serving.

Makes 10–12 servings.

Chicken Tetrazzini

Tetrazzini has become a classic American comfort food. This is a great recipe to have around after Thanksgiving to use up any left-over turkey!

1 (16-ounce) package linguine

8–12 ounces baby bella or button mushrooms, sliced

5 tablespoons butter

4 cloves garlic, minced

½ cup dry white wine

1 (10.75-ounce) can cream of celery soup

1 (10.75-ounce) can cream of mushroom soup

1 pint sour cream

½ cup milk

1 teaspoon salt

¼ teaspoon pepper

4 large chicken breasts, cooked and cubed

8 ounces Cheddar cheese, shredded (about 2 cups)

Break pasta in half, then cook in liberally salted water per manufacturer's instructions for al dente preparation. (We're just breaking it in half to make it easier to work with later.) Drain well, then set aside.

While pasta is cooking, sauté mushrooms in butter in a large skillet over medium-high heat for 4–5 minutes or until mushrooms start to brown. Add garlic; reduce heat to medium, and continue cooking for 3 minutes. Add wine to mushrooms; stir to deglaze the pan, then simmer for 6–8 minutes, or until wine is reduced by about half.

Add soups, sour cream, milk, salt, and pepper to mushrooms, and stir well. Pour mixture into a large mixing bowl. Add pasta and chicken, and stir to combine.

Pour mixture into a greased 9x13-inch baking dish, and cover with cheese. Bake uncovered at 350° for 30 minutes or until bubbly and cheese starts to brown.

Makes 8–10 servings.

Chicken Tetrazzini

Chicken Bog for a Crowd

I especially like to cook a bog when we're having any sort of party, because I can have it ready when folks arrive, then just leave it on the stove for people to serve themselves. When covered, it will stay warm for hours. I set out a stack of bowls and a bottle of hot sauce, and call 'er done!

6 large (or 8 small) chicken breasts

8 cups chicken broth

3 pounds smoked sausage

4 cups long-grain white rice, uncooked

2 teaspoons salt

2 teaspoons pepper

2 teaspoons onion powder

1 teaspoon paprika

1 teaspoon garlic powder

2 sticks butter

Add chicken and broth to an extra large pot, cover, and simmer over medium heat until chicken is cooked through. Remove chicken from pot to cool, then cut into bite-sized pieces; set aside.

Cut smoked sausage into bite-sized pieces, then add to broth. Add rice, salt, remaining spices, chicken, and butter to pot; bring to a boil. Once boiling, reduce heat to medium low, cover pot, and cook 25–30 minutes or until rice is tender, stirring only once or twice to ensure nothing is sticking to bottom of pot.

Once rice is tender, taste for seasoning, and add more salt, if desired. Turn off heat, and let chicken bog rest for 20 minutes, covered. Stir once, and serve with hot sauce, if desired.

Makes 18–20 servings.

Buffalo Feathers

I call these buffalo "feathers" because they taste just like buffalo wings but are sort of shaped like feathers! Yes, I know buffalo don't have feathers—they don't have wings either!

There's just enough brown sugar in the sauce to balance the acidic pepper sauce without being overly sweet, and the soy sauce gives it another layer of flavor.

I like to serve these with cool, crisp simple wedge salads with blue cheese dressing, because I think it just goes so perfect with the chicken!

½ cup hot sauce

1 stick butter, melted

2 tablespoons brown sugar

1 tablespoon soy sauce

½ teaspoon garlic powder

Pinch of kosher salt

2 pounds chicken tenderloins

Combine hot sauce, butter, brown sugar, soy sauce, and garlic powder in a small bowl; microwave on HIGH 45 seconds, then mix well to make the marinade and basting sauce.

Combine ⅓ cup sauce, kosher salt, and chicken tenderloins in a bowl; mix well. (I got in there with my hands to make sure all the chicken was evenly coated.) Cover; refrigerate 2–4 hours. Set remaining sauce aside, at room temperature, to baste chicken with later.

Grill chicken over medium-high heat, uncovered, until cooked through, basting 2–3 times on each side with remaining sauce. For saucier "feathers," toss with remaining sauce before serving.

Serve with celery and blue cheese dressing, if desired.

Makes 4–6 servings.

Chicken and Rice in a Bag

This is one of those fix-it-and-forget-it meals! I love to make this in the spring when we're likely to spend the whole weekend working in the yard. I can get this going and let it do its thing. The chicken cooks up moist and tender like a rotisserie chicken and is surrounded by mounds of flavorful rice!

CHICKEN SCRATCH SEASONING:

1 teaspoon salt

1 teaspoon garlic powder

1 teaspoon paprika

⅓ teaspoon white pepper

⅓ teaspoon cayenne pepper

⅓ teaspoon black pepper

⅓ teaspoon onion powder

⅓ teaspoon dried thyme

CHICKEN:

1 (4- to 5-pound) whole chicken (no larger)

1 tablespoon olive oil

1 baking bag

2 cups uncooked white rice

½ cup finely minced celery

4 cups chicken broth

1½ teaspoons salt

½ teaspoon garlic powder

Mix Chicken Scratch ingredients in a small bowl.

Rinse chicken, and remove any giblets from center cavity. Pat dry with paper towels. Rub the chicken with olive oil. Flip the chicken upside down (breast-side down), and sprinkle with a little less than half the Chicken Scratch. Flip right side up (breast-side up), and sprinkle with remaining Chicken Scratch.

Place baking bag in a 9x13-inch baking dish with open end at one of the short sides. Add rice, celery, chicken broth, salt, and garlic powder to the bag; stir to combine (or just jostle the bag around a bit). Place seasoned chicken in bag on top of rice. Puff up bag and seal with tie. Cut 3 (½-inch) slits in top of bag to vent. Place in oven, and bake at 375° for 1 hour and 20 minutes.

Remove dish from oven, and cut baking bag open. Insert a thermometer into thigh to ensure temperature is at 175°. Let rest, uncovered, 15 minutes before serving.

Makes 6–8 servings.

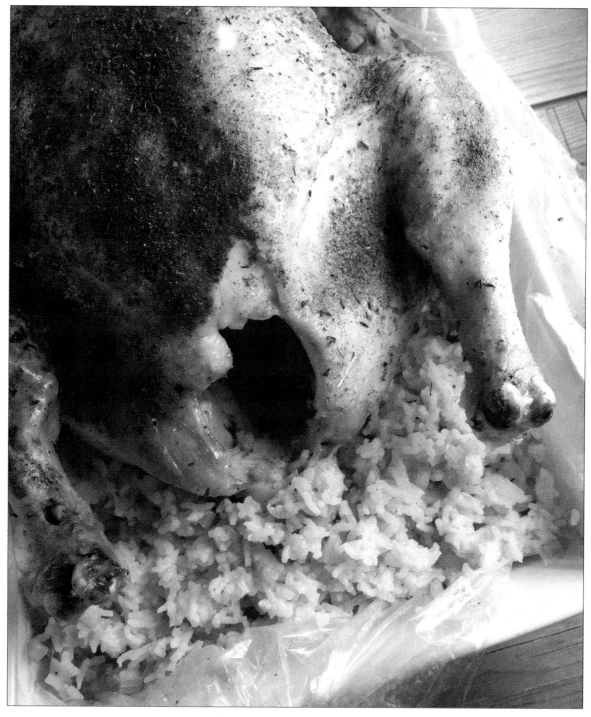

Chicken and Rice in a Bag

Country Chicken Pie

This is like a cross between Chicken Pot Pie and Chicken and Dumplings. The bottom of the biscuits stays moist—almost like a dumpling—but the top cooks up flaky like a pie crust. Underneath the biscuits is a thick, hearty chicken stew with tender chunks of chicken and hearty vegetables with a velvety gravy holding it all together. This is one of my favorite comfort foods!

4 large chicken breasts

2 cups chicken broth

½ cup water

1 teaspoon salt

2 cups each: chopped onions, celery, and carrots

6 tablespoons butter

¼ teaspoon dried thyme

½ teaspoon each: pepper and garlic powder

½ cup all-purpose flour

1 cup half-and-half

12 uncooked biscuits (canned, homemade, or frozen)

Melted butter

Cook chicken in chicken broth, water, and salt in a covered pot over medium heat until cooked through. (It's OK if the broth doesn't cover the chicken—do not add more water.) Remove chicken from stock; cool at least 10 minutes, then cut into bite-sized pieces; cover, and set aside. Reserve 2½ cups of stock.

Sauté onions, celery, and carrots in butter until onions are translucent. Add thyme, pepper, garlic powder, and flour, and stir until veggies are coated with the flour. Continue cooking and stirring for 2 minutes over medium heat.

Add reserved 2½ cups chicken stock and half-and-half to veggies, and stir continuously until smooth and thickened, 3–4 minutes. Stir in chicken until well combined.

Coat a 9x13-inch baking dish with cooking spray. Pour vegetable/chicken mixture into prepared pan. Top with biscuits, then bake, uncovered, at 375° until biscuits are golden brown on top and cooked through, 20–30 minutes for homemade or canned biscuits, and 35–45 minutes if using frozen. Remove dish from oven, then brush biscuits with melted butter. Serve and enjoy!

Makes 6–8 servings.

Perfect Steamed Shrimp

Mama and all her family are from Maryland, so I've got blue crabs and Old Bay Seasoning in my blood. I spent many a summer on the Chesapeake Bay crabbing and swimming with my grandad and cousins (all boys, by the way). Grandad was a Navy man who never could get too far away from the water. He had a houseboat on the bay, and would take us out for days at a time. We lived off of warm Shasta sodas and steamed crabs, and I still marvel at the fact none of us drowned, swimming without lifejackets, or contracted salmonella from the chicken parts we used for bait. Mama brought her love of Old Bay and prowess of steaming shellfish with her when she moved to South Carolina, and this is how she taught me to steam shrimp.

1 cup cider vinegar or strong beer

1 cup water

2 pounds large shrimp, unpeeled

¼ cup Old Bay Seasoning

Melted butter and cocktail sauce for serving

Add vinegar (or beer) and water to a large pot or Dutch oven, then bring to a boil over high heat. Liquid will be shallow.

Add shrimp to pot, then sprinkle with Old Bay. Cover, and let shrimp steam for 1 minute. Reduce heat to medium, stir shrimp well, cover again, then cook for 2–3 minutes, or until shrimp are pink in color and cooked through.

Serve hot with melted butter and/or cocktail sauce. Refrigerate leftovers. These are delicious served cold.

Makes 4–6 servings.

Easy Shrimp with Pasta

I'm so excited about sharing this recipe with you! First of all, it's crazy easy. You can totally make this on a random Tuesday night. The whole dish is done in the time it takes to cook the pasta. And don't let the list of ingredients scare you off...half of it is just spices. In a time crunch, you can use jarred blackening seasoning instead of mixing the spices.

The second thing I like is how versatile it is! I used vodka sauce when I made this batch, but I've made it with marinara sauce, too, and I loved it just as much. If you add a whack of red pepper flakes to the marinara sauce, you'll have a whole "shrimp diablo" thing going on. So good!

1 pound penne pasta (or similar shape)

½ teaspoon salt

½ teaspoon pepper

½ teaspoon cayenne pepper

1 teaspoon paprika

1 teaspoon garlic powder

1 teaspoon thyme

1 teaspoon onion powder

2–3 tablespoons vegetable or olive oil

2 pounds shrimp, peeled and deveined

1 (24-ounce) jar marinara, vodka sauce, or spaghetti sauce

¼ cup freshly grated Parmesan cheese

Chives for garnish (optional)

Cook pasta in liberally salted water per package instructions for al dente preparation. Drain pasta; set aside.

While pasta is cooking, combine salt, pepper, cayenne, paprika, garlic powder, thyme, and onion powder; toss shrimp with mixture.

Drizzle a large skillet with a little oil to coat the bottom, and heat over medium-high heat. When hot, add half the shrimp (to avoid overcrowding the pan), and sauté 3–4 minutes or until pink and cooked through. Remove shrimp from skillet; set aside. Drizzle pan with a little more oil, if necessary, and cook remaining shrimp; set aside.

Once all shrimp are cooked and removed from skillet, reduce heat to medium low, and add pasta sauce; heat through. Add pasta and half the shrimp, gently stir to combine, then pour onto a large serving plate. Arrange remaining shrimp on top of pasta; top shrimp with Parmesan cheese. Garnish with chives, if desired.

Makes 6–8 servings.

Easy Shrimp with Pasta

Browned Butter Potato-Crusted Tilapia

This recipe is based on something Mama turned me on to. She called me up one day to ask me if I had any instant mashed potato flakes. Then I just kind of stood there staring at the phone for a second because she knows I DO NOT make instant mashed potatoes. She laughed before either of us said anything else, because she knew what I was thinking. Then she went on to tell me how she'd started cooking tilapia like this and how good it was. And she was right! It's so quick and easy... and so delicious!

4–6 tilapia fillets

Salt and pepper to taste

1 cup buttermilk

2 cups instant mashed potato flakes (uncooked)

Butter

½ lemon

Season tilapia with salt and pepper; set aside.

Place buttermilk in a shallow bowl or pie plate, then place potato flakes in another shallow bowl or pie plate; set aside.

Heat butter in a nonstick skillet over medium heat until sizzling. The amount depends on size of pan—you want about ⅛ to ¼ inch butter in pan.

Dip each fillet in buttermilk, letting any excess buttermilk drip off. Next, dredge each fillet in potato flakes, shaking off any excess flakes.

Place each fillet in sizzling butter, and fry on each side 3–4 minutes, or until golden brown and crispy.

Remove fillets; squeeze lemon juice into butter in pan. Whisk until combined to make a sauce, then drizzle over fillets just before serving.

Makes 4–6 servings.

Melt-In-Your-Mouth Marinated Grilled Salmon

I LOVE this recipe! The marinade is the perfect balance of sweet, salty, and spicy, and it makes for a beautiful dark brown finish on the salmon. I like to buy a large whole salmon fillet at the wholesale shopping clubs (like Sam's or Costco), then cut it into individual servings. It's so much cheaper to buy it this way, and you can cut the portions into the size you prefer.

1½–2 pounds salmon fillets

½ cup soy sauce

⅓ cup brown sugar

¼ cup Worcestershire

¼ cup water

¼ cup vegetable oil

3 tablespoons Dijon mustard

1 teaspoon garlic powder

1 teaspoon ground ginger

1 teaspoon chili powder

Combine all ingredients, except salmon; mix well to make a marinade. Pour marinade over salmon fillets in a lidded container or large zip-top bag. Marinate in refrigerator 6–8 hours, turning occasionally so all pieces are evenly marinated.

Remove salmon from marinade, reserving marinade for basting. Grill salmon over medium heat 6–8 minutes on each side, or until fish flakes with a fork and is crispy around the edges. Baste with reserved marinade throughout cooking.

Makes 6–8 servings.

Note:

You will need to grease your grill rack before cooking. I've found the best method is to saturate a crumpled-up paper towel with vegetable oil, grasp it with a pair of tongs, then quickly grease the grill racks with the paper towel. I also like to use a greased grill pan, so I can easily remove it from the heat.

Salt and Vinegar Potato Chip Crusted Cod

You don't have to be from England to love malt vinegar with your fried fish. People in my neck of the woods love it, too! Using salt and vinegar potato chips to bread the fish gives you that yummy vinegar taste, and makes for a crunchy coating. This is so yummy and easy!

5–6 cod fillets (about 1 inch thick)

Salt and pepper to taste

1 (6-ounce) bag salt and vinegar potato chips, crushed

2 eggs

2 tablespoons hot sauce

Note:

If you don't have a baking rack, just cook fillets on a baking sheet sprayed with cooking spray, but do not coat the bottom of fillets with chips. The fish will put off moisture as it cooks, which will make for a soggy mess on the bottom if you coat it with chips and then lay directly on the baking sheet.

Line a baking sheet with aluminum foil. Place baking rack atop foil, then coat with cooking spray; set aside.

Blot fish fillets dry with paper towels, then season both sides with salt and pepper; set aside.

Place crushed potato chips in a shallow dish; set aside.

Beat eggs with hot sauce in a shallow dish; set aside.

Dip each fillet in egg wash, and let excess drip off. Place fillet in potato chips, and press down to get a good coating. Flip fillet, and coat the other side, pressing down to coat. Use a spoon to bring potato chips up to coat edges of fillet. Place on prepared baking rack. Repeat until all fillets are coated.

Bake fillets at 400° for 20 minutes or until fish is cooked through and potato chip coating is golden brown. Cool for 5–10 minutes before serving.

Makes 4–6 servings.

Beer Battered Fish

1 pound skinless cod fillets

1¼ cups all-purpose flour, divided

1¼ cups cornstarch, divided

1 teaspoon salt

1 teaspoon sugar

1 teaspoon paprika

1 (12-ounce) bottle ale or lager

1 egg, beaten

Malt vinegar (optional)

Pat fish dry with paper towels; set aside.

Heat 4 inches of oil to 350° in a large pot or Dutch oven.

Combine 1 cup flour, 1 cup cornstarch, salt, sugar, paprika, ale, and egg in a medium bowl, and mix until smooth to make a batter; set aside.

Combine remaining ¼ cup flour with remaining ¼ cup cornstarch in a shallow bowl or pie plate, and mix well. Dredge each piece of fish in flour mixture, then shake off any excess.

Dip fish into batter; fry in hot oil until golden brown and crispy. Serve with malt vinegar, if desired.

Makes 2–3 servings.

Easy Baked Fish Sticks

1 pound cod fillets, cut into strips or "sticks"

1½ cups plain dried bread crumbs

1 teaspoon salt

½ teaspoon onion powder

½ teaspoon pepper

½ teaspoon paprika

2 tablespoons vegetable oil

Combine all remaining ingredients, except fillets, in a large zip-top bag; mix well. Add 3–4 fish sticks into bag, seal tightly, then shake to coat fish with breading. Remove coated fillets, and repeat with remaining fish.

Coat a large baking sheet with cooking spray, then arrange breaded fish sticks on baking sheet. Bake at 375° for 25 minutes, or until coating is crispy and fish is cooked through.

Crispy Tuna Croquettes

My favorite way to eat these crispy gems is with fried potatoes, pork n' beans, and a whole lot of ketchup on the side! Kids love them because there aren't any chunks of onion or celery, and the inside has a nice, light consistency with a crispy outside!

3 (5-ounce) cans chunk white tuna, drained well

2 eggs, beaten

¾ teaspoon salt

½ teaspoon pepper

½ teaspoon onion powder

½ teaspoon celery seed (optional)

1 cup panko bread crumbs

Vegetable oil

Combine tuna, eggs, salt, pepper, onion powder, and celery seed in a medium bowl, and mix well. Fold in panko crumbs, and mix until just combined.

Add enough vegetable oil to a large skillet to coat the bottom, and heat over medium to medium-high heat.

Shape tuna mixture into patties about ¾ inch thick and 3 inches round. Fry in hot oil until golden brown and crispy. Drain on paper towels, and serve immediately.

Makes 3–4 servings.

Meats

Don't spend a bunch of money on your steaks—buy the inexpensive kind! It's okay. They will turn out tender and awesome if you marinate them, like I do with my Barbequed Steaks. It will change your mind about buying those more expensive thick cuts of steak.

Baked Meatballs with Mozzarella

One of my new favorite weeknight suppers is this easy recipe where the meatballs are baked in tangy marinara, and topped with gobs of buttery, gooey mozzarella. I typically serve this with some sort of hearty green vegetable like roasted Brussels sprouts or fried zucchini (instead of pasta) and some good crusty bread to soak up all that cheese and sauce.

1 (24-ounce) jar marinara sauce

20–24 Italian Meatballs, precooked (recipe below)

8 ounces mozzarella, shredded

ITALIAN MEATBALLS:

1 onion, grated

2 eggs, beaten

½ cup grated Parmesan cheese

1 teaspoon Worcestershire

1 tablespoon Italian seasoning

1½ teaspoons salt

1 teaspoon pepper

1 teaspoon garlic powder

2 pounds ground beef (80/20 works best—don't use anything too lean)

½ cup Italian dried bread crumbs

Spoon half the marinara sauce into a 9x13-inch baking dish. Arrange precooked meatballs in pan, then cover with remaining sauce. Cook, uncovered, 10 minutes at 375° or until sauce is heated through. Remove from oven, and top with mozzarella. Cook an additional 10 minutes or until cheese is bubbly and starting to brown.

Serve with pasta or hearty green vegetables.

Makes 4–6 servings.

ITALIAN MEATBALLS:

In a large bowl, combine onion, eggs, Parmesan, Worcestershire, Italian seasoning, salt, pepper, and garlic powder.

Crumble ground beef into mixture, and mix with your hands until just combined. Add bread crumbs, and continue to mix until just combined. Add more bread crumbs, if necessary, until the mixture holds together.

Turn mixture out onto a cutting board or clean counter, and shape into a rectangle. Using a sharp knife, cut mixture into 20–24 squares. Roll each square into a ball.

Line a baking sheet with aluminum foil (for easy cleanup), and spray with cooking spray. Place meatballs onto baking sheet, and bake at 400° for 18–20 minutes.

Bolognese Sauce

I need y'all to listen to me for a minute. I always thought I knew what Bolognese sauce was—just regular ol' spaghetti sauce but with more meat. I was so wrong! Bolognese sauce is more about the layering of flavors, and less about the tomatoes. You cook it for hours, uncovered, so that the sauce reduces and the flavors really intensify. When you serve it, go ahead and ladle more sauce on than you typically would with regular spaghetti sauce—so you can really enjoy it!

1 pound ground beef

1 pound ground pork

Salt and pepper to taste

1 stick butter

2 cups grated carrots

1½ cups finely diced celery

1½ cups finely diced onions

1 tablespoon minced garlic

2 cups whole milk

Pinch of nutmeg

1¼ cups dry white wine

1 (28-ounce) can crushed tomatoes

2 teaspoons Italian seasoning

1 teaspoon salt

1 teaspoon garlic powder

Note:
This is traditionally served with tagliatelle or fettucine, but any type pasta will work!

Season ground beef and ground pork with salt and pepper; brown in a Dutch oven or stockpot until cooked through. Drain, and set aside.

To the same (now empty) pot, add butter, carrots, celery, and onions; sauté over medium heat 5–7 minutes until onions are semi-translucent. Add salt and pepper to taste and minced garlic, and continue cooking for 2 minutes.

Add cooked ground meat to veggie pot; mix well. Stir in milk and nutmeg. Simmer, uncovered, over medium-low heat for 1 hour or until most liquid has evaporated. Stir occasionally, and adjust heat to maintain a very gentle simmer.

Add wine, tomatoes (with juice), Italian seasoning, 1 teaspoon salt, and garlic powder; stir well. Simmer, uncovered, over medium-low heat for 2½ hours, stirring occasionally.

Cover, and remove from heat before cooking your pasta to let the sauce rest a bit before serving.

Serve over pasta with freshly grated Parmesan cheese.

Makes 6–8 servings.

Grecian Baked Ziti

I love the combination of sauces in this recipe. The béchamel is such a creamy compliment to the zesty meat sauce. This is like a cross between pastitsio and lasagna, and makes for such a special meal! Don't let either sauce intimidate you. Both are super simple, and you'll feel like a total kitchen rock star when you're done!

1½ pounds ground beef

1 onion, diced

3–4 garlic cloves, minced

2 (15-ounce) cans tomato sauce

1½ teaspoons oregano

1 teaspoon sugar

1 teaspoon salt, divided

½ teaspoon pepper

3 tablespoons butter

3 tablespoons all-purpose flour

3 cups milk

1 cup grated Parmesan cheese

Pinch of nutmeg

12 ounces ziti, cooked and drained

2 cups shredded mozzarella cheese

Cook ground beef, onion, and garlic in a large skillet until beef is cooked through and crumbled, then drain fat.

Add tomato sauce, oregano, sugar, ½ teaspoon salt, and pepper to beef mixture; stir, then simmer over medium heat until bubbly. Remove from heat.

Melt butter in a large saucepan over medium heat. Whisk in flour, then cook 2 minutes to make a light roux. Slowly add milk to roux, whisking constantly for 5 minutes or until thickened. Stir in remaining ½ teaspoon salt, Parmesan cheese, and nutmeg, then stir well. Remove from heat.

Combine cooked ziti with Parmesan sauce, then pour into a greased 9x13-inch baking dish. Spread meat sauce evenly over ziti, then top with mozzarella.

Bake uncovered at 350° for 30–35 minutes, or until cheese is bubbly and starting to brown. Remove from oven, then rest for 15 minutes before serving.

Makes 10–12 servings.

Corned Beef and Cabbage

I serve this dish with some good crusty bread, whole-grain mustard, and dark beer!

1 (3-pound) corned beef brisket

Water

1 bay leaf (optional)

1 teaspoon whole peppercorns (optional)

Salt (½ teaspoon per every 2 cups water used)

2 pounds small potatoes, unpeeled

1 head cabbage

Place corned beef, fat side up, in large pot or Dutch oven. Add enough water to just cover brisket. Add seasoning packet from corned beef, bay leaf, peppercorns, and salt to water. Cover, and heat over medium heat until simmering. (Do NOT let water come to a full boil!) Simmer over low to medium-low heat for 2 hours. (Add 30 minutes to this cooking time for every additional pound, if cooking a larger brisket.)

Add potatoes to stock, cover, and continue simmering over low to medium-low heat for 30 minutes.

Cut cabbage into 8–10 wedges. Season wedges with salt and pepper, and arrange on top of brisket and potatoes. Cover, and continue simmering over low to medium-low heat for 30–40 minutes until cabbage is tender. (If the lid doesn't fit after you add cabbage, cover pot tightly with aluminum foil.)

Remove cabbage, potatoes, and brisket from pot, cover with foil, and let rest 10–15 minutes before serving. Cut brisket against the grain into thin slices to serve.

Makes 8–10 servings.

Chili Cornbread Pie

I love cornbread. Whenever I make chili, I always serve it with a big pan of cornbread. I break up the cornbread in the chili, and let it absorb all the yummy liquid. Another thing I like to do is crumble cornbread on top of a big chef salad. Yes, I'm serious!

Both of these notions inspired this recipe. The chili cooks on top of a cornbread crust, and is topped with creamy sour cream and melted cheese, then each serving gets piled with fresh lettuce, tomatoes, and onion. It's such a great combination!

1 (7.5-ounce) box cornbread or corn muffin mix

Ingredients needed to prepare the cornbread

1 pound ground beef

1 small onion, diced

Salt, pepper, and garlic powder to taste

1 (1-ounce) package taco seasoning

1 (15.5-ounce) can chili beans, undrained

1 cup sour cream

2 cups finely shredded Cheddar cheese, divided

Shredded lettuce, diced tomatoes, and chopped onions (optional)

Prepare cornbread batter per package instructions, and pour into a greased 8x8-inch baking dish. Bake at 400° for just 10 minutes; remove from oven. You don't want to cook all the way through.

Meanwhile, brown ground beef and onion in a medium skillet; season with salt, pepper, and garlic powder. Once meat is cooked through, drain fat. To meat mixture, add taco seasoning and undrained chili beans, and stir well. Cook until simmering, then spread chili evenly over partially cooked cornbread.

Combine sour cream and 1 cup Cheddar cheese, and mix well. Dollop on top of chili, then spread evenly over chili.

Sprinkle with remaining 1 cup Cheddar cheese, then bake at 400° for 10 minutes, or until cheese is melted.

Top each serving with shredded lettuce, diced tomatoes, and chopped onion, if desired.

Makes 4–6 servings.

Note:

Chili beans are just pinto beans with chili seasoning. If you can't find them, use a can of your favorite beans.

Chili Cornbread Pie

Smothered Salisbury Steak "Tips"

The first time I made this was out of necessity, because the ground beef I'd planned on using to make hamburger steak was still partially frozen. I decided to cut the rectangle of ground beef into squares and then treat them like meatballs. The end result was an AH-MAZE-ING gravy-smothered dish that was a cross between Salisbury steak and steak tips, so I decided to call it Salisbury Steak "Tips!"

1½ pounds ground beef

Salt, pepper, and garlic powder to taste

1 large onion, halved and sliced

2 tablespoons all-purpose flour

1 packet brown gravy mix

1⅓ cups cold water

Heat a large skillet over medium-high heat. Cut ground beef into large chunks, and season liberally on all sides with salt, pepper, and garlic powder. Add seasoned meat to hot skillet, and let sear several minutes before turning. Add onion slices around the perimeter of skillet, and season with salt and pepper.

Once meat has seared on one side, gently flip to sear on the other sides as well. (If you try to mess with the meat too much, it will crumble. Letting it sear will help keep its shape.)

Gently turn onions as you sear the meat. Once meat is seared on all (or most) sides, push meat and onions to one side of pan. Tilt pan slightly, so pan drippings come to empty side of pan. Whisk flour into pan drippings, and cook 1–2 minutes or until slightly browned. Set skillet back down flat, and reduce heat to low.

Add gravy mix to a small bowl, and whisk in water. Slowly pour gravy mixture into skillet, and stir to incorporate. Cover, and simmer over low heat 15–20 minutes, or until meat is cooked through.

Serve over mashed potatoes or rice.

Makes 4–6 servings.

Country Fried Steak with Onion Gravy

We actually just call this cubed steak, but since the rest of the free world knows it as Country Fried Steak, that's what I'm calling it here. Some folks just serve the gravy on top of the steaks (in addition to on top of rice or mashed potatoes), and some folks like to place the cooked steaks into the pan of gravy and let them simmer in it a while. It's totally up to you how to serve yours!

6–8 pieces cubed steak

1–2 cups milk or buttermilk

Salt and pepper to taste

2 cups all-purpose flour

2 teaspoons salt

1 teaspoon pepper

1 teaspoon garlic powder

½ teaspoon onion powder

Oil or shortening for frying

ONION GRAVY:

1 small onion, sliced into thin rings or diced

¼ cup pan drippings

3 cups water

Salt and pepper to taste

Cover cubed steak in milk, and marinate 2 hours. Drain steaks, then lightly season with salt and pepper; set aside.

Combine flour and remaining seasonings in a large bowl; mix well. Reserve ¼ cup flour mixture for gravy. Set aside.

Heat 1 inch of oil or shortening to 350° in a large pan or skillet.

Dredge steaks in flour mixture; fry until dark golden brown on the outside and juices run clear. Cook in batches so not to overcrowd the pan. Serve with Onion Gravy.

Makes 6–8 servings.

ONION GRAVY:

Sauté onion in pan drippings over medium heat, until onions are tender. Whisk in ¼ cup reserved flour mixture, and continue cooking 2–3 minutes until light brown. Slowly whisk in water. Cook and whisk until gravy is thickened and smooth. Add more water, if needed, to reach desired consistency. Add salt and pepper to taste.

Classic Stuffed Shells

This is a great recipe for feeding a crowd, because you can double or triple it without any special effort. The shells freeze beautifully, too, so you can make them ahead! Stuff them per the recipe, then pop them in a large zip-top bag and freeze.

10 ounces jumbo shells (approximately 20–25 shells)

1¼ pounds Italian sausage (casings removed, if applicable)

1 pound ground beef

1 (10-ounce) box frozen, chopped spinach, thawed and drained well

¾ cup grated Parmesan cheese

½ teaspoon garlic powder

¼ teaspoon salt

½ teaspoon pepper

1 (24-ounce) jar marinara sauce, divided

1 (8-ounce) can tomato sauce (garlic and/or Italian herb flavor preferred)

8 ounces mozzarella cheese, shredded

Cook shells in liberally salted water per package instructions for al dente preparation (you don't want them to be too soft, as they will continue cooking in the oven). Drain, and set aside.

Meanwhile, crumble sausage and ground beef in a large skillet, and cook until nicely browned. Drain fat, then add meat to a large mixing bowl. Add drained spinach, Parmesan cheese, garlic, salt, pepper, and ¾ cup marinara sauce; mix well.

Pour tomato sauce into a 9x13-inch baking dish. Stuff shells with sausage mixture, and arrange in a single layer in baking dish. (If you have any sausage mixture left over, just spoon it on top of or in between the shells.) Pour remaining marinara sauce over shells. Top with cheese, then bake at 350°, uncovered, 30–35 minutes, or until sauce is bubbly and cheese is melted. Rest dish, covered, for 10 minutes before serving.

Makes 5–6 servings.

Classic Stuffed Shells

Barbequed Steaks

The best thing about this recipe is that it's my granddad's creation! He was a very accomplished cook who loved to tinker in the kitchen and create his own recipes. And every time we make this, I think of him.

1 cup mustard-based barbeque sauce

1 cup traditional red (ketchup-based) barbeque sauce

1 tablespoon Worcestershire

1 tablespoon molasses

1 tablespoon honey

2 tablespoons A.1. Steak Sauce

6–8 thinly sliced sirloins or chuck steaks (½- to ¾-inch thick) cut into serving-sized pieces

Salt and pepper to taste

Combine barbeque sauces, Worcestershire, molasses, honey, and steak sauce in a large lidded container or zip-top bag. Add steaks, and marinate overnight or at least 8–10 hours.

Remove steaks from marinade, and season with salt and pepper. Reserve marinade. Grill over medium to medium-high heat until cooked through (approximately 10 minutes on each side). Baste with reserved marinade halfway through cooking time. (DO NOT cook these too hot, or the marinade will burn; there's a lot of sugar in barbeque sauce.)

Makes 6–8 servings.

Note:

Here in central South Carolina, we use mustard-based barbeque sauce a lot, so it's easy for us to find. Most grocery stores carry at least one variety of it. If you can't find it anywhere, you can order the Sticky Fingers "Carolina Classic" online.

Bull's Eye Roast with Mushroom Gravy

This is that recipe to make when the boss is coming over for dinner! It presents like something out of a five-star restaurant, it tastes gourmet, and it's practically foolproof! Any size roast between three and eight pounds will cook perfectly, since the diameter is going to be the same.

½ cup soy sauce

½ cup dry vermouth

1 tablespoon minced garlic

1 tablespoon mustard powder

1 teaspoon ground ginger

1 teaspoon dried thyme

1 (7- to 8-pound) eye of round roast

2 pounds mushrooms, sliced

2 cups water

¼ cup cornstarch

Note:

I don't recommend cooking this well done, as it will toughen the meat. The ends will be cooked through plenty if anyone is super squeamish about rare beef. You can also place meat slices in the gravy mixture (before adding cornstarch) for a minute or so to take the pink out of the roast while keeping it moist.

Combine soy sauce, vermouth, garlic, mustard powder, ginger, and thyme to make a marinade. Marinate roast in a covered bowl for 12–24 hours in refrigerator, turning occasionally.

Heat oven to 500°. Remove roast from marinade, reserving marinade in refrigerator. Place roast in a lightly greased roasting pan (on a roasting rack is preferred, but not mandatory).

Bake roast per the following chart. DO NOT open oven at all during cooking.

> 4 minutes per pound for RARE
> 5 minutes per pound for MEDIUM
> 6 minutes per pound for WELL DONE

When time is up, turn the oven off, leaving oven door closed, and let the roast slowly finish cooking for 2 hours. Again, DO NOT open oven during this time, or the roast will not cook properly.

Remove roast from pan; cover with aluminum foil.

For gravy, add mushrooms and reserved marinade to juices in roasting pan. Heat over medium-high heat on stovetop. Once simmering, cook and stir 5 minutes or until mushrooms are tender. Whisk water with cornstarch, then add to pan. Cook 3–4 minutes or until gravy thickens.

Makes 10–16 servings.

Egg Roll Stir-Fry

This recipe has all the flavor of an egg roll without the wrapper! It's like an unstuffed egg roll in a bowl. I love to make this when I'm trying to cut carbs. I make a big batch on Sunday, then heat up the leftovers throughout the week for delicious, fun lunches!

1 pound ground beef or pork

1 large onion, diced

1 small head cabbage

3 carrots

4–5 cloves garlic, minced

1 tablespoon grated fresh ginger

½ teaspoon black pepper

2 tablespoons sesame oil

1 tablespoon vegetable oil

¼ cup soy sauce

Cook and crumble ground meat with onion in a very large skillet until meat is cooked through. Do not drain. You'll need to select a skillet large enough to contain all the cabbage—divide everything evenly into two skillets, if necessary.

While meat and onions are cooking, cut cabbage into thin shreds; set aside.

Peel carrots with a vegetable peeler, then either dice small, or use the peeler to shave off thin slices; set aside.

Combine garlic, ginger, pepper, sesame oil, vegetable oil, and soy sauce in a small bowl; set aside.

Add cabbage and carrots to ground meat, then cook and stir over medium-high heat for 3–4 minutes. Add soy sauce mixture, and stir well.

Reduce heat to medium, and continue cooking for 5–10 minutes or until cabbage is tender.

Makes 4–6 servings.

Egg Roll Stir-Fry

Slow Cooker Carnitas

True carnitas cook in lard like a confit, but...ain't nobody got time for that! Or, should I say...ain't nobody got two gallons of lard for that? I think this comes pretty dang close to the real thing, since the roast slowly cooks in its own rendered liquid.

You can feed a lot of people with this with very little effort, so it's one of my go-to recipes for entertaining. I serve it with guacamole, pico de gallo, and salsa, set out a giant bowl of tortilla chips, and call 'um in.

1 teaspoon salt

1 teaspoon cumin

1 teaspoon cayenne pepper

1 teaspoon chili powder

1 teaspoon oregano

½ teaspoon onion powder

½ teaspoon black pepper

1 (6- to 7-pound) Boston butt or pork shoulder roast

1 tablespoon vegetable oil

1 lime

Combine salt and spices in a small bowl. Rub the roast with oil, then coat with spice mixture. Cover and refrigerate to marinate in the spices overnight (8–10 hours).

Cook roast (without adding water) in slow cooker on HIGH for 6 hours or LOW for 10 hours.

Remove roast from slow cooker, cover, and let rest 30 minutes. Meanwhile, pour rendered cooking liquid into a measuring pitcher, and let sit until liquid and fat have separated. Spoon fat off, and set aside.

Roughly chop roast into chunks, and spread onto a baking sheet lined with aluminum foil. Cut lime into wedges or chunks, and squeeze juice all over pork. (I toss squeezed lime pieces into pan with pork for extra flavor.)

Drizzle ⅓ cup of rendered fat over pork. Place baking sheet on middle oven rack, and broil on high until pork pieces begin to sizzle and crisp up. Remove from oven, and serve.

Tip:

Serve carnitas as is, or assemble into soft tacos using heated soft flour tortillas. I usually top mine (as is, or as a taco) with diced onion, chopped cilantro, avocado slices, and freshly squeezed lime juice.

Perfect Pork Tenderloin

This tenderloin is one of my go-to dishes to serve when we're having company. It has a slight Asian zing to it, which I love, because I think Asian-inspired marinades go perfectly with pork! If we have any leftovers, I like to cut the meat into small cubes and use it in fried rice the next day!

2 pork tenderloins

4 cloves garlic, minced

1 teaspoon grated fresh ginger, or ¼ teaspoon ground

½ teaspoon black pepper

3 tablespoons brown sugar

¼ cup soy sauce

2 tablespoons Dijon mustard

1 teaspoon sesame oil

2 tablespoons vegetable oil

GLAZE:

2 tablespoons brown sugar

1 tablespoon Dijon mustard

1 tablespoon soy sauce

Rinse tenderloins under cold water. Pat dry, and add to a gallon zip-top bag or sealable container; set aside.

For marinade, combine garlic, ginger, black pepper, brown sugar, soy sauce, and mustard in a small bowl, and mix well. Whisk in sesame oil and vegetable oil until mixture is emulsified (oil isn't separated from liquid). Pour marinade over tenderloins; refrigerate 8–12 hours.

Spray a baking dish with cooking spray. Arrange tenderloins in baking dish; pour marinade over tenderloins. Bake, uncovered, at 350° for 30 minutes.

Combine Glaze ingredients, and brush over both tenderloins. Return tenderloins to oven, and continue cooking 5–10 minutes, or until cooked to desired temperature:

Medium rare–145°
Medium–150°
Well done–160°

Remove from oven, cover loosely with aluminum foil, and rest 5–10 minutes before serving.

Makes 6–8 servings.

Spicy Pork

We rarely go out to eat these days. And when we do, we always have the kids with us, so the hip little Korean place isn't exactly where we go anymore. That's unfortunate, because their Spicy Pork is one of my favorite foods ever! So I figured out how to make it at home! The first time I made it, we ate all of it and were looking for more!

As the name implies, this is spicy. You might want to be mindful who you serve it to if they're sensitive to spicy heat.

1 (1- to 1½-pound) pork tenderloin

5–6 green onions

1 tablespoon Sriracha (red chili pepper sauce)

1 tablespoon soy sauce

¼ teaspoon black pepper

¼ teaspoon salt

Vegetable oil

SAUCE:

3 tablespoons Sriracha

2 tablespoons soy sauce

1 tablespoon barbeque sauce

1 tablespoon sugar

2 teaspoons minced garlic

½ teaspoon sesame oil

½ teaspoon ground ginger

Cut tenderloin in half lengthwise. Slice each strip very thinly. Place in a medium bowl; set aside.

Chop green onions into 2-inch pieces, reserving ends to be chopped as garnish later. Add onion pieces, Sriracha, soy sauce, pepper, and salt to pork; stir to combine. Cover, and marinate 2–8 hours in refrigerator.

Combine Sauce ingredients; stir well; set aside.

Add just enough oil to coat bottom of a very large nonstick skillet or wok; heat over high heat. Add half the pork and onions in a single layer (cook in batches). Cook 3–5 minutes, stirring frequently, or until nicely browned and starting to crisp. Remove to a bowl or plate, and continue cooking remaining pork and onions. Once all pork is browned, return to skillet; reduce heat to medium, add Sauce, and stir to coat. Continue cooking 3–4 minutes, or until sauce is thickened.

Serve with white rice, and garnish with reserved chopped green onions. (This cooks quickly, so be sure rice is almost done before cooking the pork.)

Makes 3–4 servings.

Spicy Pork

Easy Baked Country Ribs

Country ribs (sometimes referred to as "country-style" ribs) are just slabs cut from the sirloin or rib end of the pork loin, which are cut into rib-shaped slices (most often boneless). I love to use them because they're inexpensive, tender, and meaty.

When I'm looking for a no-muss, no-fuss meal, I love to throw these in the oven, let them cook low and slow, then douse them with barbeque sauce at the end. They are as tender as butter and will just fall apart if your fork even looks at them hard. And they're impossible to mess up.

2 pounds country ribs

Salt and pepper to taste

½ cup barbeque sauce

Season ribs liberally with salt and pepper on all sides (feel free to jazz up your spices, but I tend to like plain ole salt and pepper on these). Arrange ribs evenly in a 9x13-inch baking pan. Cover pan tightly with aluminum foil or a tight-fitting lid, and bake at 250° for 3 hours.

Remove ribs from oven, and increase temperature to 400°. Baste ribs with your favorite barbeque sauce, and cook, uncovered, 5–10 minutes, or until sauce is heated through and starting to get a little sticky.

Makes 4–6 servings.

Fall-Off-The-Bone Baby Back Ribs

These ribs cook low and slow in the oven on a bed of thick onion slices to keep them out of the pan juices (so they roast, instead of boil). Finish them off with barbeque sauce, and you're ready to chow down.

Come to find out, I was cooking them almost exactly the way they cook them at some restaurants. Yay! I love it when I figure this stuff out on my own. And it sure beats standing out in the heat, sweating buckets, and swatting mosquitoes for hours.

2 racks baby back ribs (or back ribs)

Salt and pepper to taste

Garlic powder

Paprika

3–4 onions, peeled

½ cup beer or water (approximately)

2 teaspoons liquid smoke (optional)

Barbeque sauce

Season both sides of ribs liberally with salt, pepper, garlic powder, and paprika; set aside.

Slice onions into ½-inch rings, and place in bottom of a large roasting pan (or 2 smaller pans).

Pour just enough beer or water into pan to cover bottom. (I once used a hard apple cider; use whatever you have.) Add a few drops of liquid smoke to the beer.

Arrange rib racks in a single layer on top of onion slices. Cover pan tightly with 2 layers of aluminum foil. Bake at 300° for 4 hours. Remove ribs from oven, and uncover.

Drain pan juices from pan (either with a turkey baster, or by carefully tipping the pan). Baste ribs with barbeque sauce, and return to oven. Continue baking ribs, uncovered, for 15 minutes. Remove ribs from oven, tent with foil, and let rest 15 minutes before serving.

Makes 4–6 servings.

Pierogi and Sausage Skillet

I didn't grow up knowing what a pierogi was, but in that stretch of my life that encompassed broke college life and broke early career life, I became very cozy with them! These affordable little wonders are dumplings filled with mashed potatoes. This is a dish I like to make that dresses up the pierogi with smoky kielbasa, onions, and cheese. Everyone loves it!

1 (1-pound) box potato pierogi

1 pound kielbasa

1 tablespoon vegetable oil

2 onions

½ cup butter

Salt and pepper to taste

2 cups shredded Cheddar cheese

Sour cream (optional)

Cook pierogi in boiling salted water per package instructions, then drain well.

Meanwhile, cut kielbasa into bite-sized pieces, then sauté in vegetable oil in a large skillet until nicely browned. Remove kielbasa from skillet; set aside.

Cut onions into rings, then sauté in skillet with butter until onions are light golden brown.

Add cooked pierogi, sausage, salt, and pepper to skillet, and stir until well combined, and pierogi are coated in butter.

Sprinkle cheese over pierogi mixture in skillet, and continue cooking on medium low until cheese is melted.

Serve with sour cream, if desired.

Makes 4–6 servings.

Italian Sausage and Pasta with Tomato Cream Sauce

This is an insanely delicious and easy pasta dish with Italian sausage and creamy tomato sauce that tastes like something that took all day to prepare!

I love to make this when we're having company, because it's so easy to double (or triple). Sometimes I cook the sausage ahead of time, then just assemble the rest of the recipe once everyone's ready to eat. I like to serve this with a green salad and crusty Italian bread.

8 ounces bow tie pasta

1¼ pounds hot Italian sausage (casings removed, if applicable)

1 (14-ounce) can petite diced tomatoes, drained well

1 teaspoon dried oregano

½ teaspoon garlic powder

½ teaspoon salt

½ pint (1 cup) heavy cream

¼ cup freshly grated Parmesan cheese

Cook pasta in liberally salted water per package instructions, then drain well.

Meanwhile, brown and crumble sausage in a large skillet over medium-high heat until sausage is cooked through. (Drain your sausage at this point if you have an excessive amount of rendered fat.)

Add drained tomatoes, oregano, garlic powder, and salt, and stir well. Add cream, and bring to a slight boil. Reduce heat to medium, and simmer uncovered for 8–10 minutes or until sauce is reduced and thickened.

Remove skillet from heat, then add cooked pasta and Parmesan cheese. Stir to combine. Serve with additional Parmesan cheese, if desired.

Makes 4–6 servings.

Bubble-Up Pizza with Sausage

Who needs delivery pizza when you can whip this up so quickly? This reminds me of a deep-dish pizza, because the dough is so fluffy, and it's all covered with gobs of buttery, delicious melted mozzarella! Feel free to add whichever pizza toppings you enjoy, like olives, pepperoni, and green bell peppers.

1¼ pounds hot or mild Italian sausage (casings removed, if applicable)

Olive oil

1 (15-ounce) can refrigerated biscuits (8-count)

Garlic powder and kosher salt to taste

2 tablespoons shredded Parmesan cheese

1 (24-ounce) jar marinara sauce

3–4 cups shredded mozzarella cheese, divided

Fresh basil leaves, rolled and sliced thin (optional)

Break sausage into bite-size pieces with your fingers. Add sausage pieces to a large skillet, and brown over medium-high heat until cooked through, leaving them in small pieces so they resemble little meatballs. Set aside.

Drizzle a 9x13-inch baking dish with a little olive oil. Use your hands or a paper towel to spread oil in bottom of pan to coat well.

Unwrap biscuits, then cut each biscuit into 4 pieces. Place biscuit pieces in greased baking dish. Sprinkle dough with garlic powder, salt, and Parmesan cheese.

Pour marinara sauce over dough. Arrange sausage pieces over sauce, then top with half of the mozzarella. Bake uncovered at 350° for 15 minutes. Remove from oven; top with a little fresh basil and remaining mozzarella. Continue baking, uncovered, for 20–25 minutes or until cheese is bubbly and starting to brown.

Serve with more fresh basil, if desired.

Makes 8–10 servings.

Bubble-Up Pizza with Sausage

Cajun Beans and Rice

Those of you who have been with me for a while know how much I love rice. We eat more rice in my family than potatoes and grits combined. Yeah, for real! We don't usually eat mashed potatoes and gravy like everybody else; we eat rice and gravy. And I love to scramble up a couple eggs in leftover rice for breakfast! SO of course, I love this dish and make it often.

1 (20-ounce) bag Cajun 15 Bean Soup mix

1 onion, diced

6 cups chicken broth (see note)

2 cups water

2 pounds andouille sausage or smoked sausage

Cooked long-grain white rice

Combine beans (with included seasoning packet), onion, chicken broth, and water in a large pot or Dutch oven. Heat over medium-high heat until simmering. Once simmering, cover pot, then reduce heat to low, and simmer 3 hours.

Cut sausage into bite-sized pieces; add to beans. Continue cooking beans 2–3 more hours or until beans are tender. If desired, you can thicken your beans by simmering over medium heat with lid off for 20–30 minutes.

Remove from heat, cover, and let beans rest for 30 minutes before serving. Serve over white rice.

Makes 16–18 servings.

Notes:

• This finishes a little on the salty side due to the broth, seasoning packet, and sausage, which is exactly how I like it when serving it over plain white rice. If you're looking to cut down on salt, use low-sodium chicken broth, or water.

• If you can't find andouille in your market, substitute with smoked sausage or kielbasa, or ham.

• If you can't find Cajun-flavor 15 Bean Soup mix, use the regular 15 Bean Soup mix, then add Cajun spices.

Cakes

Well, some things are just hard to make a recipe out of. Like buttercream frosting. I just keep adjusting the ingredients until it looks right. But that doesn't help you much, now does it? So I finally fiddled with the recipe long enough to get it down into writing. Now it's foolproof. When I'm in a hurry, I just whip up some boxed cupcakes and layer on this frosting. It's so good, everyone thinks I made the whole thing from scratch.

Springtime Pistachio Cake

If you like Watergate Salad, you'll love this recipe! The cake is rich and light, which is a hard combo to come by. The club soda is surely what contributes to the lightness of it, and the pudding mix is what helps make it so rich. I love to make this at Easter, because the light green color just says springtime to me!

1 box white cake mix

1 small box pistachio instant pudding mix

1 cup vegetable oil

3 eggs

1 cup club soda

½ cup finely chopped pecans or pistachios

FROSTING:

2 envelopes Dream Whip whipped topping mix

1 small box pistachio instant pudding mix

1½ cups milk

¼ cup finely chopped pecans or pistachios

Combine cake ingredients; mix at medium speed with an electric mixer 3 minutes.

Pour batter into a greased and floured Bundt pan; bake at 350° for 40–45 minutes, or until toothpick inserted in the middle comes out clean.

Cool for 10 minutes in the pan; turn out onto a serving plate. Cool cake completely.

FROSTING:

Combine Dream Whip with pudding mix in a medium-size mixing bowl. Slowly add milk, and beat with an electric mixer on low speed until combined. Increase mixer speed to high, and beat 4–6 minutes or until soft peaks form.

Spread Frosting evenly over cooled cake. Garnish with finely chopped pecans or pistachios. Refrigerate cake until ready to serve.

Makes 12–14 servings.

Hummingbird Cake

3 cups all-purpose flour

2 teaspoons baking soda

1 teaspoon salt

1 teaspoon cinnamon

2 cups sugar

3 eggs

1¼ cups vegetable oil

2 teaspoons vanilla extract

1 (8-ounce) can crushed pineapple, undrained

2 ripe bananas, mashed with a fork

1½ cups finely chopped pecans, divided

1 cup flaked coconut (optional)

CREAM CHEESE FROSTING:

2 (8-ounce) packages cream cheese, softened

2 sticks butter, softened

2 teaspoons vanilla extract

4 cups powdered sugar, sifted

Sift together flour, baking soda, salt, and cinnamon; set aside.

Combine sugar, eggs, oil, and vanilla; beat on medium-low speed with an electric mixer until creamy. Slowly mix in flour mixture until just combined.

Add pineapple, bananas, 1 cup chopped pecans, and coconut; continue mixing on medium-low speed until all ingredients are thoroughly combined, about 1 minute.

Pour cake batter into 3 greased and floured 9-inch cake pans; bake at 350° for 20–25 minutes or until cakes are cooked through. Cool completely.

Frost with Cream Cheese Frosting. Sprinkle remaining ½ cup chopped pecans over cake. Store in refrigerator.

Makes 12–14 servings.

CREAM CHEESE FROSTING:

Whip cream cheese, butter, and vanilla with an electric mixer until fluffy, about 2 minutes. Beat in powdered sugar gradually (add more, if necessary to reach spreadable consistency).

Mama's Red Velvet Cake

Most modern versions of red velvet cake have cream cheese frosting, and since I never met a cream cheese frosting I didn't like, that's A-OK with me. But our old-fashioned family recipe uses what some folks call a "cooked" icing. It's very stable, and doesn't have to be refrigerated (though, you can if you want). It stands up to humidity and fluctuating temperatures like we're prone to here in the South. If you're looking for a true, authentic, southern red velvet cake recipe, this is it!

1 stick butter, softened

1½ cups sugar

2 eggs

2 tablespoons cocoa powder

1 (1-ounce) bottle red food coloring

1 teaspoon salt

2 teaspoons vanilla extract

1 cup buttermilk

2¼ cups cake flour

1½ teaspoons baking soda

1 tablespoon vinegar

COOKED BUTTERCREAM ICING:

5 tablespoons cake flour

1 cup milk

2 sticks real, salted butter, softened

1 cup sugar

1 teaspoon vanilla

Cream together butter and sugar with an electric mixer on medium speed until light and fluffy. Add eggs, 1 at a time, mixing well after each addition.

Mix cocoa powder and food coloring in a small bowl to make a paste; add to butter mixture, and mix until well combined.

Mix salt, vanilla, and buttermilk in a small bowl; add to butter mixture alternately with cake flour. Mix well.

Mix baking soda and vinegar in a small bowl; fold into batter by hand until well combined.

Pour batter into 2 greased and floured 9-inch cake pans; bake at 350° for 30 minutes or until cooked through. Cool completely, then frost.

Makes 8–10 servings.

COOKED BUTTERCREAM ICING:

Put flour in a small saucepan, then whisk in milk. Heat over medium-high heat until boiling. Cook and stir until thickened (about consistency of cake batter). Remove from heat, and cool completely.

Cream butter and sugar with an electric mixer 3–4 minutes until fluffy. Add vanilla and cooled flour mixture, and continue mixing until creamy and spreadable. This takes a while—just keep mixing!

Mama's Red Velvet Cake

No-Fail Vanilla Buttercream Frosting

I love this recipe. It uses a one-pound box of powdered sugar, so there's no need to measure! The only variance is whether you need three or four tablespoons of milk or cream, and that's really about preference and climate. I usually use milk, because it's what I have, but cream makes for a more luxurious, silky buttercream, so I definitely recommend using it, if you have it!

1 stick salted butter, softened

1½ teaspoons vanilla extract

3–4 tablespoons milk or cream

1 (1-pound) box powdered sugar

Whip butter and vanilla on medium speed with an electric mixer until smooth and creamy (about 1 minute). Mix in 3 tablespoons milk or cream; gradually add powdered sugar, mixing on medium speed 2–3 minutes until well combined and fluffy. Add more milk or cream, 1 teaspoon at a time, until you reach your desired consistency.

Yields enough for 24 normal cupcakes, or 16 heavily frosted cupcakes, or a 9x13-inch cake. If you're making a layer cake, double the recipe to ensure you have enough.

Variation:
Make chocolate frosting by adding ⅓ cup cocoa powder when you add the powdered sugar. You'll need about a teaspoon more milk or cream.

Mama's Blue Ribbon Kahlúa Cake

This is my mom's signature cake. Everybody, and I do mean everybody, *asks for this cake for any special occasion. Mama entered it in a big-to-do local cake contest, and won first prize! This recipe makes enough icing to ice two cakes, but I'm not mucking around with the recipe because it's Mama's. I'd suggest making two cakes!*

1 box devil's food cake mix

½ cup sugar

⅓ cup vegetable oil

3 eggs

¾ cup water

¼ cup bourbon

½ cup Kahlúa

¾ strong black coffee

2 teaspoons cocoa powder

ICING:

1 stick butter

1 cup sugar

¾ cup evaporated milk

1½ cups chocolate chips

Combine ingredients in a large bowl, and mix on low speed with an electric mixer 4 minutes.

Pour batter into a greased and floured Bundt pan. Bake 45–50 minutes or until cooked through. Cool cake in pan; invert onto a cake stand or serving plate.

ICING:

Heat butter, sugar, and evaporated milk in a saucepan over medium heat until boiling. Boil 2 minutes, then remove from heat.

Stir in chocolate chips, and continue stirring until chips are completely melted. Slowly pour hot Icing over cake.

Makes 14–16 servings.

Honest-To-Goodness Lane Cake

Lane Cake is a true southern heirloom recipe that dates back over 100 years ago when it won the blue ribbon in an Alabama county fair.

1 cup butter, softened

2 cups sugar

3½ cups all-purpose flour

1 tablespoon baking powder

½ teaspoon salt

1 cup milk

1 teaspoon vanilla

8 egg whites

FILLING:

1 cup raisins

½ cup butter, melted

8 egg yolks

1 cup sugar

1 cup sweetened flaked coconut

1 cup chopped pecans

½ cup bourbon

1 teaspoon vanilla extract

FROSTING:

3 egg whites

1½ cups sugar

⅓ cup water

1 tablespoon bourbon

Cream butter and sugar with an electric mixer 3–4 minutes until fluffy. Sift together flour, baking powder, and salt; add slowly, alternating with milk; add vanilla. Mix on low until just combined.

Beat egg whites on high until stiff peaks form. Gently fold into batter, half at a time.

Pour into 3 greased and floured 9-inch cake pans. Bake at 325° for 20–25 minutes. Cool in pans 10 minutes; turn out onto wire racks to cool completely.

Makes 12–14 servings.

FILLING:

Place raisins in a bowl; cover with boiling water. Let stand 30 minutes; drain well.

Combine melted butter, egg yolks, and sugar in a saucepan; cook and stir over medium-low heat, 12–15 minutes until thick. Remove from heat; stir in rehydrated raisins, coconut, pecans, bourbon, and vanilla. Cool completely.

Place 1 cake layer on cake plate. Spread with ⅓ of the Filling. Repeat layers twice.

FROSTING:

In bottom of double boiler, bring 2 inches of water to a low boil. In top of double boiler, combine all ingredients with electric mixer on low. Increase speed to high, and mix 7–10 minutes until spreadable. Spread Frosting up side of cake, leaving fruit filling visible in center of top layer. Store cake in an airtight container.

Honest-To-Goodness Lane Cake

Peanut Butter Sheet Cake

2 cups all-purpose flour

2 cups sugar

1 teaspoon baking soda

1 teaspoon salt

2 sticks butter

1 cup water

1 cup peanut butter

½ cup milk

1 teaspoon vanilla

2 eggs

FROSTING:

1 stick butter

½ cup peanut butter

⅓ cup milk, plus more, if needed

1 pound powdered sugar

Combine flour, sugar, baking soda, and salt in a large bowl; set aside.

Combine butter, water, and peanut butter in a saucepan; heat over medium heat until boiling, stirring constantly. Pour into flour mixture.

Add milk, vanilla, and eggs to bowl with peanut butter and flour mixtures, and stir by hand with a large sturdy spoon until well combined and smooth.

Pour mixture into a greased and floured 10x15-inch pan (or 2 smaller pans); bake at 350° for 25–35 minutes or until cooked through. Cool completely in pan.

Makes 20–24 servings.

FROSTING:

Combine butter, peanut butter, and ⅓ cup milk in a saucepan, and heat over medium heat until boiling, stirring constantly.

Remove from heat; stir in powdered sugar until smooth, adding more milk, 1 teaspoon at a time, until desired consistency is achieved.

Immediately pour Frosting over cake. Let cake sit until cool before serving. Store in an airtight container.

Cherry Dump Cake

We've all had dump cakes, but this one is a little different than what you may be used to. This one eats more like a cobbler. The fruit stays moist and velvety, and the cake and almonds cook up golden and delicious.

Recipes like this are perfect when you want to whip up something quick or serve something hot out of the oven when you're entertaining.

1 (21-ounce) can cherry pie filling

1 (20-ounce) can crushed pineapple in syrup, undrained

1 box yellow cake mix

1 stick butter, melted

1 cup (4 ounces) sliced almonds

Dump cherry pie filling into a 9x13-inch baking dish; spread evenly. Dump (spoon) crushed pineapple (with juice or syrup) evenly on top of pie filling. Dump (sprinkle) cake mix evenly over fruit.

Drizzle melted butter over dry cake mix; top with sliced almonds. Bake at 350° for 45 minutes.

Serve hot with ice cream, or cold with whipped cream, or just enjoy it as is!

Makes 16–18 servings.

Variations:

Feel free to substitute different types of nuts or pie filling! I love this with blueberries and walnuts, too.

Lemon Crumble Cream Cake

1 white cake mix

Egg whites, oil, and water for mix

1 lemon, zested and juiced

½ cup sugar

1 stick butter, melted

1½ cups all-purpose flour

Pinch of salt

1 (8-ounce) package cream cheese, softened

2 cups powdered sugar, plus more for dusting

1 cup heavy whipping cream

Prepare cake batter per package instructions. Stir in lemon zest. Pour into a greased and floured 10-inch springform pan.

Combine sugar, melted butter, flour, and salt in a small bowl; stir with a fork until combined and crumbly; sprinkle over batter. Bake at 350° for 35–45 minutes or until cooked through. Cool completely; slice in half horizontally.

Combine cream cheese, powdered sugar, and lemon juice in a large bowl; mix until well combined and smooth.

In a separate bowl, beat whipping cream until soft peaks form. Fold whipped cream into cream cheese mixture until well combined.

Spread cream cheese mixture over bottom half of cake; top with remaining half of cake. Dust top of cake liberally with powdered sugar. Refrigerate until ready to serve.

Makes 12–14 servings.

Lemon Crumble Cream Cake

Black Bottom Cupcakes

Because these cupcakes didn't have sprinkles or mounds of icing or cherries on top, or flaming sparklers stuck in them, I didn't pay them too much attention to them as a kid. Now as an adult, I totally get it. They're not overly sweet—in the best way. The chocolate cake is rich and dark, and centered in the middle is a dollop of chocolate chip cheesecake!

1 (8-ounce) package cream cheese, softened

1 egg

⅛ teaspoon salt

¼ teaspoon vanilla extract

⅓ cup sugar

1 cup miniature semisweet chocolate chips

1 box chocolate cake mix

Black coffee, cold

Oil and eggs to make the cake

In a medium bowl, beat cream cheese, egg, salt, vanilla, and sugar with an electric mixer until smooth and creamy. Stir in chocolate chips; set aside.

Prepare cake batter per package instructions, substituting black coffee for water.

Place cupcake liners in cupcake/muffin pan, and spray lightly with cooking spray. Fill liners ⅓ full with cake batter. Dollop—don't press down—1 heaping tablespoon of cream cheese mixture onto cake batter.

Bake at 350° for 20 minutes, or until toothpick inserted into cake comes out clean. Cool to room temperature, then refrigerate in an airtight container.

Makes 28–30 servings.

Easy Pineapple Upside-Down Cake

1⅓ sticks butter, melted

1¼ cups brown sugar

1 (20-ounce) can pineapple slices

Maraschino cherries, drained

1 yellow cake mix

Eggs and oil for mix

Note:

If reserved pineapple juice does not equal the amount of water called for on package directions, add enough water to compensate.

Pour butter into a 9x13-inch baking pan; sprinkle brown sugar evenly on top of butter.

Reserving juice, arrange pineapple slices in pan. Add a cherry to center of each pineapple ring, and in between adjoining rings.

In large bowl, prepare cake mix according to package directions, using reserved pineapple juice in place of water; mix on medium speed 2 minutes.

Carefully pour batter over pineapples. Bake at 350° for 35–40 minutes or until cake is cooked through. Let cake rest 5 minutes. Run a knife along edges to loosen, if necessary; invert cake onto a platter or cookie sheet. Serve warm or softened. Store in an airtight container. Makes 12–14 servings.

Vanilla Wafer Cake

2 sticks butter, softened

2 cups sugar

6 large eggs

1 teaspoon vanilla extract

1 (11-ounce) box vanilla wafers, finely crushed

½ cup milk

1 (8-ounce) bag sweetened flaked coconut

1 cup chopped pecans

Cream butter, sugar, and eggs with an electric mixer 2–3 minutes until light and fluffy. Add remaining ingredients, and mix well.

Pour into a greased and floured Bundt pan; bake at 350° for 1 hour or until toothpick inserted in the middle comes out clean.

Cool in pan 15 minutes, then turn out onto a cake stand or serving plate. Store in an airtight container.

Makes 10–12 servings.

Chocolate Nutter Butter Icebox Cake

There's a barbeque joint down the road called Little Pigs that I love to visit. I can't go there often, because I eat like a little pig when I go in there. They've got a buffet a mile long with every southern side under the sun. And they usually have two desserts: banana pudding (of course), and an AH-MAZE-ING chocolate dessert with peanut butter cookies that inspired this recipe.

It takes a lot longer for Nutter Butters to soften up using cold pudding, so I decided to use cook-and-serve pudding in this recipe to really soften those cookies up and make them more cake-like. I also wanted to sweeten the pudding a little, since the Nutter Butter cookies aren't super sweet, and I knew I could do that easily with cooked pudding.

2 (3.4-ounce) boxes chocolate cook-and-serve pudding mix

4 cups milk

½ cup sugar

1 teaspoon vanilla

Pinch of salt

1 (1-pound) package Nutter Butter cookies (peanut butter sandwich cookies)

1 (8-ounce) carton Cool Whip, thawed

¼ cup peanut butter

Combine pudding mixes, milk, sugar, vanilla, and salt in a medium saucepan. Bring to a boil over medium heat, stirring constantly. Once softly boiling, remove from heat.

Spoon ⅓ of the warm pudding into bottom of an 8x8-inch baking dish. Add a single layer of cookies over pudding. Pour another ⅓ of pudding over cookies; add another single layer of cookies. Top with remaining ⅓ of pudding. Let rest 30 minutes, then refrigerate until completely chilled, 6–8 hours or overnight.

Top with Cool Whip. Melt peanut butter for 20–30 seconds in the microwave, and stir until thin enough to pour. Drizzle over Cool Whip, and serve. Cover and refrigerate to store.

Makes 14–16 servings.

Chocolate Nutter Butter Icebox Cake

Strawberry Cream Cheese Icebox Cake

This beauty is one of my most-requested recipes ever! It's a cross between Strawberry Shortcake and Cheesecake, so it tastes fresh and light, but still super luxurious. Plus, it travels great and can be prepared a day in advance, so I tend to make this quite a lot for picnics, potlucks, and holiday dinners!

2 pounds strawberries

2 sleeves graham crackers, divided

1 (8-ounce) package cream cheese, softened

1 (14-ounce) can sweetened condensed milk

2 (3.4-ounce) packages cheesecake-flavored instant pudding mix

3 cups milk

1 (12-ounce) carton Cool Whip, thawed, divided

Clean strawberries and slice about ¼ inch thick; set aside. (Do this first—the cream cheese mixture will set up quickly once mixed.)

Line bottom of 9x13-inch baking dish with graham crackers (save some for topping); set aside.

Beat cream cheese and sweetened condensed milk with an electric mixer until smooth and creamy. Stir in pudding mixes and milk; continue mixing on low 4–5 minutes until mixture starts to thicken. Fold in 2 cups Cool Whip until smooth.

Pour half of cream cheese mixture over graham crackers. Arrange a single layer of strawberry slices over cream cheese mixture (about half). Top strawberries with another layer of graham crackers, then cover with remaining cream cheese mixture. Cover and refrigerate 6–8 hours.

When ready to serve, add another layer of strawberries; top with remaining Cool Whip. Crush remaining graham crackers, and sprinkle over top.

Makes 24–28 servings.

Cookies & Candies

Most brownie recipes make small batches. And lemme tell you something…I'm not turning my oven on for one little 8x8-inch pan of brownies. If I'm cranking that puppy up, I'm getting my money's worth. So what if there's leftovers. My Fudgy Cocoa Brownies are just as good the next day.

Cake Mix Cookies

This is the easiest recipe ever! When you want to whip up something quick for holiday baking and want to have a large variety of cookies without huge batches (or effort), these are perfect!

I used the caramel-filled Nestle Toll House DelightFulls, because Husband laid an egg when he spotted them in the grocery store (he has serious issues with caramel). And also because I figured it would be the perfect amount of chips for this size batch of batter, but you can absolutely use 1½ cups of chocolate chips or other morsels.

2 eggs

½ cup vegetable oil

1 box chocolate cake mix

1 (9-ounce) package Nestle Toll House DelightFulls milk chocolate morsels with caramel filling (or 1½ cups regular chocolate chips)

Note:
Use any flavor cake mix and any type of chips or morsels for this recipe.

Add eggs and oil to a large bowl or stand mixer, and mix well. Add dry cake mix, and mix on low until well combined, about 1 minute. Stir in morsels or chocolate chips.

Refrigerate batter 30 minutes to firm up a bit. Roll batter into 1-inch balls; place on cookie sheet 2 inches apart. Bake at 350° for 8–9 minutes or until set. (Chill batter between batches to make sure it doesn't get too soft.)

Makes 38–40 cookies.

Chewy Peanut Butter Cookies

I like to make this batter the day before I plan on baking, because you have to refrigerate the dough anyway. I'll whip up the batter, toss it in the fridge, then make quick work out of baking the cookies the next day. You'll want to have two baking sheets when you make these to save time, since you need to let the cookies rest a bit when you pull them out of the oven.

2 sticks butter, softened

1 cup sugar

¾ cup brown sugar

2 eggs

1 teaspoon vanilla extract

1 cup creamy peanut butter

3¼ cups self-rising flour

Note:

You can line your cookie sheets with nonstick coated aluminum foil for all your cookies—no need to spray or grease at all.

In a mixing bowl, cream together butter, sugar, and brown sugar with an electric mixer 3–4 minutes or until light and fluffy. Add eggs, vanilla, and peanut butter; mix until well combined.

Combine flour with peanut butter mixture, and mix on low speed until combined. Dough will be thick. Cover, and refrigerate 2 hours (or overnight).

Shape dough into 1-inch balls, and place on a greased baking sheet about 2 inches apart. Press down slightly to flatten height by a third. You can use the traditional "back of the fork" trick, or use the back of 3 fingers for a smoother finish.

Bake at 350° for 8–10 minutes or until just starting to brown on bottom. Cool cookies IN THE PAN for 10 minutes before moving to a cooling rack or plate to cool completely. Cookies may seem too soft or undone until completely set. Store in an airtight container.

Makes 28–30 cookies.

Cookie Sandwiches with Creamy Marshmallow Frosting

When you make cookie sandwiches, you need a frosting with a little more body and elasticity than a traditional buttercream to physically support the cookies, and to withstand a bite without shooting out the sides. This no-fail frosting is beautiful and pipes like a dream! I don't think it tastes like marshmallows; it's just this fluffy, light, crisp-white frosting that is insanely delicious!

48–50 chocolate chip cookies, baked and cooled

No-Fail Marshmallow Cream Frosting (recipe below)

Sprinkles (optional)

CREAMY MARSHMALLOW FROSTING:

1 (7-ounce) jar marshmallow crème, or marshmallow "fluff"

2 sticks salted butter, softened

1 teaspoon vanilla extract

2–3 teaspoons milk or cream

1 (1-pound) box powdered sugar

Flip half of cookies upside down. Pipe frosting onto back of cookies going about ⅛ inch from edge. Place remaining cookies on top of frosting to make cookie sandwiches. Press down slightly until frosting spreads to edges. Roll edges of cookie sandwiches in sprinkles, if desired. Store in an airtight container at room temperature for up to 1 week.

FROSTING:

Whip marshmallow crème, butter, and vanilla on medium speed with an electric mixer until well combined and fluffy, about 2 minutes. Add 2 teaspoons milk or cream and powdered sugar; mix on medium speed until smooth. Add more milk or cream, ½ teaspoon at a time, if necessary, until you reach your desired consistency.

Makes 24 servings.

Note:

I don't bother with a piping bag and fancy tip. I just load up a zip-top bag and snip off a tip bit of one corner. And when I'm done, I throw the bag in the trash. Boom. Done.

Cookie Sandwiches with Creamy Marshmallow Frosting

Butterscotch Haystacks

The first time I made these for the family, no one could remember what they were called! Brutus and Husband were having a particularly hard time with it, and I laughed at their expense for a straight week! They called them fence posts, hay bales, scarecrows, barn doors, farm boys, straw stumps, and more that I can't even remember.

2 (11-ounce) bags butterscotch morsels

¾ cup peanut butter

2 teaspoons vegetable oil

1 (5-ounce) can chow mein noodles

1¼ cups salted dry-roasted peanuts

Note:

You can omit the peanuts and double the chow mein noodles for traditional haystacks

Gently melt butterscotch morsels, peanut butter, and vegetable oil over medium-low heat in a saucepan (or in a double-boiler), stirring constantly, until morsels have melted and mixture is smooth.

Add noodles and peanuts to a large bowl. Pour butterscotch mixture over noodles and peanuts, and gently stir until everything is evenly coated.

Use 2 spoons to drop little "haystacks" of mixture onto wax paper or parchment paper. Leave haystacks to firm up for approximately 4 hours. Once set, store at room temperature in an airtight container.

Makes 40–42 servings.

Oatmeal Scotchies

Butterscotch is one of my all-time favorite flavors for making cookies! I think the hearty, rustic oats go so well with the sweet, buttery butterscotch morsels. These travel really well, so if you want to send someone a care package, or bring something sweet along with you on a little trip, these are perfect!

2 sticks butter, softened

¾ cup sugar

¾ cup brown sugar

2 eggs

2 teaspoons vanilla extract

1¼ cups all-purpose flour

1 teaspoon baking soda

½ teaspoon salt

3 cups quick oats (uncooked)

1 (11-ounce) package butterscotch chips (about 1⅔ cups)

In a mixing bowl, cream together butter, sugar, and brown sugar with an electric mixer for 3–4 minutes or until light and fluffy. Add eggs and vanilla; mix until well combined.

Combine flour, baking soda, and salt in a small bowl. Add to butter mixture, and mix on low speed until combined. Using a sturdy wooden spoon, stir in oats and butterscotch chips.

Drop by rounded tablespoons onto an ungreased cookie sheet about 2 inches apart. Bake at 375° for 7–9 minutes, or until lightly brown around bottom. Cool in pan 2–3 minutes, then move to a cooling rack or plate to cool completely. Store in an airtight container.

Makes 40–45 cookies.

Chex Scotcheroo Bars

Scotcheroos are one of my favorite treats, because they have chocolate AND peanut butter AND butterscotch in them, and that's a culinary perfect storm. They're typically made with crispy rice cereal (not Chex), but the Chex cereal has a slightly roasted flavor that really stands up well to the sweet chocolate and butterscotch!

6 cups Corn Chex cereal

1 cup light corn syrup

1 cup sugar

2 cups peanut butter, divided

1 teaspoon vanilla

¼ teaspoon salt

1 (12-ounce) package semisweet chocolate chips

1 (11-ounce) package butterscotch morsels

Coat a 9x13-inch pan very lightly with cooking spray; set aside. Coat a large mixing bowl very lightly with cooking spray, then add cereal to bowl; set aside. (You need to do both of these steps first, because you need to work pretty quickly once your syrup mixture is ready, or it will start to set up.)

Combine corn syrup and sugar in a medium pan; cook over medium heat until boiling, stirring occasionally; remove from heat. Add 1½ cups peanut butter, vanilla, and salt; stir until smooth.

Pour corn syrup mixture over cereal in prepared bowl; gently fold until combined. Spread mixture into prepared pan. (The mixture doesn't need to be pressed down flat, just relatively even.)

Combine chocolate chips, butterscotch morsels, and remaining ½ cup peanut butter in a medium microwave-safe bowl; heat approximately 1½ minutes until melted, stopping every 30 seconds to stir until smooth and creamy; pour over cereal mixture.

Cool, uncovered, until set; cut into squares.

Makes 24–28 servings.

Reese's Pieces Peanut Butter Bars

The middle layer in these bars is like silky peanut butter fudge, and it is AH-MAZE-ING! Especially if you like waking up at 1:30 a.m. to slip downstairs and have one with a cold glass of milk...and you don't even realize you did it until you wake up in the morning to find crumbs on the counter and an empty glass and your husband looking at you like he's thinking about planning some sort of intervention! True story.

2 sticks butter, melted

1 cup brown sugar

½ teaspoon baking soda

1 teaspoon salt

1½ cups all-purpose flour

2¼ cups quick-cooking oats

½ cup creamy peanut butter

1 (14-ounce) can sweetened condensed milk

1 (10.5-ounce) bag Reese's Pieces candies (about 1½ cups)

Variation:

You can substitute M&M's for the Reese's Pieces. I like to make them with seasonal colored M&M's for whichever holiday is upon us!

Line a 9x13-inch baking pan with aluminum foil, then coat with cooking spray; set aside.

Combine melted butter, brown sugar, baking soda, and salt in large bowl; mix with electric mixer on low speed until smooth. Add flour and oats; continue mixing until well combined. Reserve 1 heaping cup oat mixture; press remaining into bottom of prepared pan. Bake at 350° for 10 minutes.

In a small bowl, mix peanut butter and condensed milk until smooth. Pour mixture over semi-cooked oat crust, and spread evenly over crust.

Sprinkle half reserved oat mixture over peanut butter mixture. Top with Reese's Pieces; sprinkle remaining oat mixture on top of candies. Continue baking 25 minutes, or until oat crumbles begin to brown.

Cool completely in pan, then remove by lifting up aluminum foil. Cut into bars, and store in an airtight container.

Makes 24–28 servings.

Salted Caramel Turtle Bars

I love these bars! You won't believe how easy the are to make, and they look and taste like something from a la-tee-da bakery!

SHORTBREAD CRUST:

1 stick butter, softened

2 cups all-purpose flour

¼ cup sugar

TURTLE BARS:

1 heaping cup coarsely chopped pecans

½ teaspoon kosher salt or coarse-grain salt

2 sticks butter

⅔ cups sugar

1 (12-ounce) package semisweet chocolate chips

SHORTBREAD CRUST:

Combine butter, flour, and sugar; beat on low with an electric mixer (or paddle attachment, if using a stand mixer) until incorporated, and dough sticks together when squeezed between your fingers. (Shortbread doughs are dry and meal-like. As long as it holds when you pinch it together, you're good to go.)

Press shortbread dough evenly into the bottom of an ungreased 9x13-inch baking pan.

TURTLE BARS:

Sprinkle pecans and kosher salt over crust; set aside.

To make the caramel, combine butter and sugar in a medium saucepan; heat over medium heat until boiling, stirring occasionally. Once boiling, continue cooking for exactly 3 minutes. Pour caramel evenly over pecans, without scraping the bottom of saucepan. Bake at 350° for 14 minutes.

Remove from oven, then sprinkle chocolate chips over caramel. Wait 5 minutes for chocolate to melt, then spread evenly over caramel layer.

Once cool and chocolate is set (it takes forever to set…sorry about that), cut into squares. Store in an airtight container.

Makes 20–24 servings.

Chewy Chocolate Chip Cookie Bars

Since I don't usually have time to sit around waiting for three to four pans of cookies to bake, THIS is how I like to make chocolate chip cookies! Throw all the batter in a 9x13-inch pan, and go for broke! If you're looking for Valentine's, Christmas, or any other themed cookies, just throw a handful of seasonal M&Ms on top before baking, and you're golden!

1½ sticks butter, mostly melted

¾ cup sugar

¾ cup brown sugar

2 eggs

1½ teaspoons vanilla extract

2¼ self-rising flour

1 (12-ounce) bag semisweet chocolate chips (2 cups), divided

Line a 9x13-inch baking pan with aluminum foil, then spray lightly with cooking spray; set aside. Preheat oven to 350°.

Combine butter and sugars in a stand mixer or large bowl, and mix until smooth. Mix in eggs and vanilla until well combined.

Add flour, and mix on low speed until combined. Stir in all but about 3 tablespoons of chips.

Spread dough evenly into prepared pan, then sprinkle reserved chocolate chips on top.

Bake at 350° for 25–30 minutes or until light golden brown around the edges.

Once cool, lift aluminum foil to remove cookie slab from pan. Cut into 24 bars; store in airtight container.

Makes 24 servings.

Note:

You don't have to fool with reserving the handful of chocolate chips to sprinkle on top; it's just a little trick food bloggers and food stylists use for swanky "chippage." Otherwise, all chips are mixed in the batter, and you don't really see them much. If you're using M&Ms, just sprinkle on top.

Man Bars

I call these Man Bars, because they're so easy to prepare, even a man can make them. HA HA!! Stop. Don't send me hate mail. I'm kidding!

I love these so much, because, besides being so easy, a man can make them...they travel well, they're not overly sweet (no, seriously, they're not), everyone I've served these to LOVES them, and they're just so different!

1 (14-ounce) box graham crackers (3 sleeves), crushed into crumbs

1 (12-ounce) bag semisweet chocolate chips

1 cup finely chopped walnuts or pecans

2 (14-ounce) cans sweetened condensed milk

1½ teaspoons vanilla extract

½ teaspoon salt

2–3 cups powdered sugar

Combine graham cracker crumbs (about 4 cups total), chocolate chips, nuts, condensed milk, vanilla, and salt in a large bowl, and mix until well combined to make a batter.

Line a 3-quart, 9x13-inch baking pan with parchment paper (or greased aluminum foil), then spread batter into pan. Bake at 350° for 30 minutes or until set.

Cool completely in pan, remove, and cut into squares. Add powdered sugar to a medium bowl, and add squares; toss to coat. Store in an airtight container.

Makes 44–48 squares.

Note:

When you make these, try to find good quality, traditional graham crackers (not cinnamon or chocolate flavored), because one of the things I like most about them is the flavor from the graham crackers.

Fudgy Cocoa Brownies

Nothing beats a homemade brownie. Don't get me wrong, there are some pretty good box mixes out there—but none of them are as good as chewy, gooey, glorious homemade brownies. But many recipes are just too fussy. I want to open up my cabinet, pull out a few ingredients, and make some simple, super easy brownies.

I sift the cocoa with the flour, because cocoa tends to clump. I use a combo of butter and oil because each brings something to the table—the rich flavor from the butter and the moisture from the oil.

1⅓ cups all-purpose flour

¾ cup unsweetened cocoa powder

1 teaspoon salt

½ teaspoon baking soda

2 eggs

⅓ cup vegetable oil

⅓ cup butter, melted

2 cups sugar

1 teaspoon vanilla extract

½ cup black coffee, at room temperature (can substitute water)

1 cup semisweet chocolate chips (optional, but amazing)

1 cup chopped nuts (optional)

Sift together flour, cocoa powder, salt, and baking soda; set aside.

In a large mixing bowl, combine eggs, oil, melted butter, sugar, vanilla, and coffee; beat on low speed with an electric mixture until smooth. Slowly add flour mixture, and mix until just combined. Stir in chocolate chips and nuts, if desired.

Coat a 9x13-inch baking pan with cooking spray, then spread batter evenly in pan. Bake at 350° for 35–40 minutes, or until toothpick inserted in the middle comes out clean.

Makes 24–28 servings.

Mud Hen Brownies

These brownies have got to be one of the neatest recipes I've ever made. Whenever I bring them to a potluck, everybody's always like, "What in the world is that?!" The meringue topping is just too cool, and really makes for a unique experience. It's crispy and chewy at the same time. It's like an epicurean oxymoron. Ha! See there Mrs. Jowers, I was paying attention in English! You really didn't need to make me sit in the hall. All the time. Because I was talking constantly. Even when you moved my desk. Three times.

1 family-size box brownie mix (for 9x13-inch pan)

2 eggs, separated

1 cup semisweet chocolate chips

1 cup mini-marshmallows

1 cup chopped nuts

1 cup brown sugar

Coat a 9x13-inch baking pan with cooking spray; set aside.

Prepare brownie batter per package instructions for oil and water, but not eggs. Use 2 egg yolks ONLY (if your brownie mix calls for 3 eggs, only use 2 yolks, and add 1 tablespoon water). Reserve egg whites for meringue. Spread batter into prepared pan.

Top brownie batter evenly with chocolate chips, marshmallows, and nuts.

In a cold, clean mixing bowl, beat egg whites on high speed with an electric mixer until stiff peaks form. Fold in brown sugar, and stir until smooth and there are no lumps. Spread mixture evenly over nuts.

Bake at 350° for 20 minutes, then cover pan loosely with aluminum foil (just lay a sheet over the pan—don't seal it), and continue baking for 20 more minutes, or until brownies are cooked through.

Remove from oven, uncover, and cool for 1 hour before serving. Store in an airtight container.

Makes 24–28 servings.

Sno Ball Brownies

My love for coconut knows no end. So of course I love Sno Ball snack cakes—chocolate cake stuffed with white icing, dipped in this marshmallow stuff, and coated in hot pink coconut. Why hot pink? I have no idea.

These are my version of that tasty snack, made with brownies instead of cake. I love how when you cut these, the squares mound and sort of take the rounded shape of the original!

1 family-size box brownie mix (for 9x13-inch pan)

1 (16-ounce) can vanilla cake frosting

1 (7-ounce) jar marshmallow crème, or marshmallow "fluff"

3 cups sweetened flaked coconut

4–8 drops pink food coloring

Note:

If you prefer homemade, you can use my No-Fail Marshmallow Cream Frosting (page 166) instead of the can of prepared frosting, mixed with the marshmallow crème.

Bake brownies according to package instructions in a 9x13-inch pan, and cool completely.

Combine frosting and marshmallow crème in a bowl, mix well, then spread over brownies.

Place coconut in a bowl, and squeeze in 2 drops food coloring. Use a fork to "tumble" the coconut around in the bowl until the color is evenly distributed. Add more food coloring, 2 drops at a time, until coconut is bright pink.

Sprinkle coconut over frosting; cut and serve. Store at room temperature or in refrigerator (per preference) in an airtight container.

Makes 24–28 servings.

Cherry Cheese Danish Bars

These bars taste just like a cherry cheese Danish, but are super easy to make and store. The flaky tender crust is so delicious with the creamy filling and sweet cherries. I use almond extract in these, because it really highlights the natural flavor of the cherries. These are awesome to make when company's coming! They are so AH-MAZE-ING with a hot cup of tea or coffee!

3 cups all-purpose flour

1 teaspoon baking powder

1 teaspoon salt

2 sticks butter, softened

2¼ cups sugar, divided

5 eggs, divided

1 teaspoon vanilla extract

1 (8-ounce) package cream cheese, at room temperature

2 (21-ounce) cans cherry pie filling

1 cup powdered sugar

½ teaspoon almond extract

2–3 tablespoons milk

Combine flour, baking powder, and salt in a medium bowl, and stir to incorporate; set aside.

Cream butter and 2 cups sugar for 2 minutes with electric mixer. Add 4 eggs and vanilla; mix until combined. Gradually add flour mixture, and mix until all ingredients are incorporated to form a dough.

Grease a 10x15-inch pan, then press half the dough into bottom of pan. Cover with wax or parchment paper, then use your hands to spread the dough evenly.

Combine cream cheese, remaining egg, and remaining ¼ cup sugar; beat with an electric mixer until smooth. Spread over dough. Spoon cherry pie filling evenly over filling.

Dollop small spoonfuls of remaining dough evenly on top until all dough is used. Bake at 350° for 35–45 minutes until golden brown. Cool completely.

Combine powdered sugar, almond extract, and 2 tablespoons milk to make a glaze thin enough to pour (add more milk, if necessary). Drizzle glaze over bars; cut into squares. Store at room temperature in an airtight container.

Makes 28–32 servings.

Cherry Cheese Danish Bars

Snickerdoodle Bars

I love Snickerdoodles! But sometimes I just want something easy, and the idea of throwing this batter together in one pan is right up my alley! These are just as chewy and delicious as the traditional cookies—but so much easier!

2 sticks butter, softened

2 cup plus 2 tablespoons sugar, divided

1½ teaspoons cinnamon, divided

¾ teaspoon salt

2 eggs

2 teaspoons vanilla extract

2 cups all-purpose flour

Cream butter and 2 cups sugar with an electric mixer 2–3 minutes or until fluffy. Add ½ teaspoon cinnamon, salt, eggs, and vanilla; mix well. Add flour, and mix until just combined.

Butter a 9x13-inch baking pan, then spread dough evenly into pan. Mix remaining 2 tablespoons sugar and 1 teaspoon cinnamon together, then sprinkle evenly over dough. Bake at 350° for 30–35 minutes, or just until edges start to brown.

Cool completely in pan, then cut into squares to serve.

Makes 24–28 squares.

Best Ever Rice Krispies Treats

These aren't your plain-Jane, back-of-the-box Rice Krispies Treats. These are rich and luxurious and vanilla-y, because they have extra butter and double the marshmallows and vanilla! If you want to win the bake sale, this is how you do it. And if you really want to blow everybody's mind, add sprinkles to the top before they set up. Patsy PTA's store-bought cupcakes ain't got nothing on these babies.

10 cups crispy rice cereal

1 stick real, salted butter

1½ teaspoons vanilla extract

¼ teaspoon salt

2 (10-ounce) bags miniature marshmallows, divided

Measure exactly 10 cups of rice cereal, and pour into a large mixing bowl; set aside.

Line a 9x13-inch baking pan with aluminum foil; spray lightly with cooking spray, and set aside.

Melt butter over low heat in large pot. Add vanilla, salt, and all but 2 cups marshmallows. Cook and stir over low heat until marshmallows are completely melted. Once mixture is smooth, add remaining 2 cups marshmallows, and stir to incorporate. (Marshmallows will mostly melt, but those little lumps that are left are going to add little pockets of marshmallow awesomeness to the treats.)

Immediately pour marshmallow mixture over rice cereal, and gently stir until evenly coated.

Spread mixture into prepared pan. (I use a rubber spatula to get it level, then use another 9x13-inch pan to smoosh everything down nice and evenly.) Let cool to room temperature, uncovered. Once set, remove from pan by lifting up aluminum foil; cut into 24–30 squares. Store in an airtight container.

Makes 24–28 servings.

Lemon Crumb Squares

1 (14-ounce) can sweetened condensed milk

½ cup lemon juice

1 teaspoon lemon zest

1½ cups all-purpose flour

1 teaspoon baking powder

½ teaspoon salt

1⅓ sticks butter, softened

1 cup sugar

1 cup oatmeal

Mix sweetened condensed milk, lemon juice, and lemon zest in small bowl until well combined; set aside.

In a separate bowl, sift together flour, baking powder, and salt; set aside.

In a large mixing bowl, beat butter and sugar with an electric mixer until light and fluffy. Add flour mixture and oatmeal, and mix until crumbly.

Press half of crumb mixture into a greased 9x13-inch pan, covering bottom completely to make a crust. Pour lemon mixture evenly over crust, then sprinkle with remaining crumb mixture.

Bake at 350° for 25 minutes, or until edges start to brown. Cool in pan completely, then cut into squares. Store in an airtight container.

Makes 24–28 squares.

Salted Almond Chocolate-Covered Toffee

Candy making has always scared me a bit, because it seems there are just too many things that have to be perfect. But this recipe has never failed! I don't have to use a candy thermometer. I just cook it until it's the color of, well, toffee.

2 sticks real butter

1 cup sugar

½ teaspoon vanilla

¼ teaspoon salt

1 (12-ounce) bag semisweet chocolate chips (about 2 cups)

⅓ cup chopped roasted almonds

A few pinches of coarse-grain or kosher salt

Tips:

Don't stir this too fast or the toffee could "break" when the oil in the butter separates from the rest of the mixture. If it seems your toffee is "breaking," stop stirring for 15-second intervals.

Scrape the bottom of the pan while stirring, so no "hot spots" develop.

Line 9x13-inch pan with aluminum foil; set aside.

Heat butter, sugar, vanilla, and ¼ teaspoon salt in a heavy-bottom saucepan over medium heat until butter is melted, stirring slowly with a wooden spoon. Increase temperature slightly, and slowly stir until mixture starts to boil. Once boiling, continue cooking and slowly stirring for about 7 minutes, or until light brown in color (or 290° on candy thermometer, if you go that route).

Without scraping bottom of saucepan, pour toffee into prepared pan, and spread evenly using a rubber spatula. (Work quickly, as toffee will start to set up.) Wait 1 minute, then sprinkle chocolate chips evenly over hot toffee. Wait another 1–2 minutes for chocolate to get soft, then spread evenly over toffee. Sprinkle chopped almonds and coarse-grain salt on top.

Let rest, uncovered, at room temperature until chocolate is set. (Once cool, you can refrigerate for 10–15 minutes to help the chocolate set more quickly—no longer, or condensation will form.)

Once everything is completely firm, lift foil to remove toffee slab from pan. Cut into pieces using a sharp knife (the more imperfect, the better, I think!). Store in an airtight container.

Makes 20–24 servings.

Grandma Betty's Peanut Butter Fudge

This recipe makes the best peanut butter fudge I've ever had! I like that you can really taste the peanut butter. As the name implies, it was my Grandma Betty's recipe, and it's coming to you from an old, splatter-covered, worn-out, yellowed piece of notebook paper the recipe was written on over 20 years ago.

1 pound powdered sugar

½ cup milk

1 (7-ounce) jar marshmallow crème

1 cup peanut butter

Line an 8x8-inch pan with parchment or aluminum foil. Spray lightly with cooking spray; set aside.

Combine powdered sugar and milk in a medium saucepan, and heat over medium heat until boiling. Boil 2 minutes; remove from heat.

Add marshmallow crème; stir well. Add peanut butter; stir until well combined.

Pour into prepared pan, and allow to rest until firm. Once firm, remove from pan and cut into squares.

Makes 36–38 pieces.

Pies & Other Desserts

Y'all, I love banana pudding so much, I couldn't decide which recipe to include here. So guess what? I added them all! Each one is different but equally good. Now you get to decide which one you love the most!

Simply Southern Sweet Potato Pie

Definitely bake your sweet potatoes, rather than peeling and boiling them—it really intensifies the flavor and makes for a silkier consistency in the pie filling. When sweet potatoes are in season, I like to bake more than what the recipe calls for. Then I can pop the extras in the fridge (once they're cool), and reheat them in the microwave for a quick side dish anytime!

1 pound sweet potatoes

1 stick butter, softened

1 cup sugar

2 eggs

½ cup milk

¼ teaspoon nutmeg

¼ teaspoon cinnamon

¼ teaspoon salt

1 teaspoon vanilla extract

1 (9-inch) pie crust

Pierce sweet potatoes with a fork; bake on a foil-lined pan, uncovered, at 375° for 45 minutes to an hour, or until soft on the inside. Cool potatoes to room temperature; using your fingers, peel off skin.

Put potatoes in a mixing bowl; beat with an electric mixer until smooth. (If your sweet potatoes have any fibrous "strings," the beaters will catch them, and you can easily discard so your pie isn't stringy.)

Mix in butter, sugar, and eggs until smooth. Add milk, nutmeg, cinnamon, salt, and vanilla, mixing again until smooth.

Pour filling into pie crust; bake at 350° for 50–60 minutes, or until edges of pie filling just start to brown. Cool pie completely before serving. Store in an airtight container (at room temperature or refrigerated—whichever you prefer).

Makes 8–10 servings.

Old-Fashioned Buttermilk Pie

2 cups sugar

½ cup butter, softened

3 eggs, room temperature

¼ cup all-purpose flour

1 cup buttermilk

1 teaspoon vanilla extract

¼ teaspoon salt

1 (9-inch) pie crust, unbaked

½ teaspoon cinnamon (optional)

In a large mixing bowl, cream sugar and butter with an electric mixer until light and fluffy. Add eggs; mix well. Add flour, buttermilk, vanilla, and salt; mix until smooth.

Pour batter into pie crust; dust with cinnamon, if desired. Bake at 350° for 1 hour and 10 minutes, or until toothpick inserted in center comes out clean. (The center will still be a little jiggly; don't worry…it will set up!)

Remove pie from oven; cool completely. Store in an airtight container at room temperature.

Makes 6–8 servings.

Eggnog Pie

When I start seeing eggnog in the store, I know it's Christmastime! I love to put eggnog in my coffee, heat it up like hot cocoa, drink it with a splash of spiced rum, or just drink it straight up. I love it so much, I decided to make a pie with it! This recipe makes two pies, so you can freeze one for later, after the eggnog disappears.

2 (3.4-ounce) boxes vanilla instant pudding mix

1 teaspoon nutmeg

1 quart (4 cups) eggnog

1 (12-ounce) tub Cool Whip, thawed, divided

2 (9-inch) graham cracker pie crusts

Put pudding mix and nutmeg in a large mixing bowl. Pour in eggnog, and mix on low speed 2 minutes. Fold in half the Cool Whip. Divide mixture evenly into graham cracker crusts. Cover and refrigerate 6 hours or until set.

Serve with remaining Cool Whip. Garnish with a dusting of nutmeg, if desired.

Makes 2 pies: 8–10 servings each.

Sugar Cream Pie

You know what I love about this pie? Well, first, let's state the obvious: it's pie. Amen? I love this pie, because it's perfectly imperfect. When it's just about done, a couple of big ole bubbles form on the top. They deflate or pop or do whatever bubbles do when they're done being bubbles. And then this wonky, almost whimsical, beautiful caramel-colored imperfection is left on top.

1 cup sugar

2 tablespoons all-purpose flour

¼ teaspoon salt

1 teaspoon vanilla

2 cups heavy whipping cream

1 (9-inch) pie shell (not deep dish), thawed

Whipped cream for serving

Combine sugar, flour, and salt in a large bowl; mix with wooden spoon or rubber spatula. Break up any lumps or clumps. Add vanilla and cream; stir 1 minute or until sugar is somewhat dissolved. (Do not use a whisk or electric mixer, as we do not want to whip the cream before cooking.)

Pour cream mixture into pie shell. Place on middle rack in oven; place a larger pan on rack below pie to catch any spills. Bake at 400° for 20 minutes. Cover edges with aluminum foil or a crust guard. Rotate pie 180° (just to make sure it bakes evenly), and continue baking 25–30 minutes, or until edges of cream start to caramelize. (It will still be jiggly; that's okay!)

Cool to room temperature, then cover and refrigerate at least 4 hours or until set. Serve with fresh, slightly sweetened whipped cream. (I just buy a quart of cream when I make this, so I have enough for pie and for topping.)

Makes 8–10 servings.

Sugar Cream Pie

Sour Cream Raisin Pie

If you want to make something different for Thanksgiving or Christmas, definitely give this vintage pie a try. It has all the warm notes of a pumpkin or apple pie, so it'll feel like the holidays, but it won't be the same-ole, same-ole! The sour cream cooks up almost like a caramel, the raisins plump up and get all lovely, and the whole thing is wrapped in a warm blanket of cinnamon and nutmeg.

2 cups sugar

2 cups sour cream

2 eggs, beaten

3 tablespoons all-purpose flour

1½ teaspoons vanilla extract

½ teaspoon salt

½ teaspoon cinnamon

½ teaspoon nutmeg

1 (12-ounce) box raisins (approximately 2 cups)

1 cup chopped walnuts or pecans (optional)

2 (9-inch) deep-dish pie crusts, cooked

1 (8-ounce) carton Cool Whip

Additional cinnamon for dusting

Combine sugar, sour cream, eggs, flour, vanilla, salt, cinnamon, and nutmeg in a large saucepan; stir until smooth.

Add raisins, and heat and stir over medium heat until slightly boiling. Reduce heat to medium low; simmer, stirring occasionally, 5 minutes or until mixture has thickened.

Stir in nuts, if desired, then divide filling evenly into pie shells. Cool 10 minutes, then refrigerate, uncovered, until cold.

When ready to serve, spread Cool Whip evenly over pies, and dust with cinnamon. (I usually do this with a small mesh strainer for a more even and delicate dusting.)

Cover and refrigerate to store.

Makes 2 pies: 8–10 servings each.

Atlantic Beach Pie

This North Carolina coast specialty is like a taste of the beach. Seriously! If you could put salt and sun in a pie, it would taste like this! It's made with a creamy, tart lemon filling in a crunchy, thick saltine cracker crust, and topped with whipped cream and sea salt.

1½ sleeves regular saltine crackers (not unsalted)

3 tablespoons sugar

1 stick butter, softened

4 egg yolks

1 (14-ounce) can sweetened condensed milk

½ cup lemon juice

Whipped cream

Coarse-grain sea salt

In a large bowl, crush crackers with your hands just until all crumbs are pea-sized or smaller (you want a chunky meal, not a fine crumb). Add sugar and butter, and knead with your hands until crumbs begin to stick together. (Things will be crumbly. It's okay.)

Press crust on the bottom, up the side, and onto rim of 8-inch pie plate. Refrigerate 15 minutes, then immediately bake at 350° for 15 minutes.

Once crust is out of oven, make filling (not sooner, as it will begin to set once you mix it up).

Combine egg yolks, sweetened condensed milk, and lemon juice; mix until smooth. (You can do this by hand with a large whisk, or use an electric mixer on medium speed. Don't mix more than 2 minutes total, or the filling will be too thick.)

Pour filling into crust (does not have to be cooled). Bake at 350° for 15–17 minutes, or until set.

Cool for 30 minutes at room temperature, then refrigerate 4–6 hours, or until pie is completely cold. Serve topped with whipped cream and sprinkled with coarse-grain sea salt.

Makes 8–10 servings.

Butterfinger Pie

Sometimes I shy away from recipes that are as easy as this one, because I pride myself on having a knack for recipe development. But y'all! This one is too good not to share. It's light and fluffy and rich and decadent at the same time. And it's crazy easy. This freezes beautifully, so consider making two, and saving one for later!

14 ounces Butterfinger candy bars

1 (8-ounce) package cream cheese, softened

½ teaspoon vanilla extract

1 (12-ounce) container Cool Whip, thawed

1 (9-inch) graham cracker crust

Chop Butterfingers into small bits, and set aside, reserving ½ cup to sprinkle on top of pie. (I've done this a few ways over the years, and have found the best way is to just line them up on a cutting board and chop with a chef's knife. Using a food processor or smashing with a mallet or rolling pin tends to cream the chocolate a bit, and things start to clump together.)

Beat cream cheese and vanilla with an electric mixer until fluffy. Add half the Cool Whip, and mix until smooth.

Fold in crushed Butterfingers and remaining Cool Whip; mix by hand until evenly combined. Spoon mixture into pie crust. Sprinkle reserved ½ cup chopped Butterfingers over pie. Cover; refrigerate 2 hours before serving. Store in refrigerator.

Makes 8–10 servings.

Note:

Use any size Butterfinger candy bars (snack sized, fun sized or standard), so long as you have about 14 ounces total.

Pig Pickin' Pie

You know that Mandarin orange cake with the fluffy pineapple frosting that goes by the name of Pig Pickin' Cake? I'm addicted to that frosting. It's super light and fluffy, and delicious all by itself. So I got to thinking about making a dessert out of just the frosting. And it turned out way better than I imagined! The light, fluffy, sweet filling is perfect with the buttery, slightly salty cracker crust! I call this Pig Pickin' Pie, in honor of the cake.

2 sleeves (about 60) Ritz Crackers, crushed

1 stick butter, melted

¼ cup sugar

1 (20-ounce) can crushed pineapple in heavy syrup, undrained

1 (5.1-ounce) package vanilla instant pudding mix

1 (16-ounce) carton Cool Whip, thawed

Combine crushed crackers, melted butter, and sugar; mix well. Press firmly into bottom of a 9x13-inch baking dish, or in bottom and up the side of 2 (9-inch) pie plates; set aside.

In a large bowl, mix together crushed pineapple (with syrup) and pudding mix. Fold in Cool Whip until well combined. Spoon pie filling evenly over crust(s). Cover; refrigerate 4–6 hours before serving.

Makes 20–24 servings.

No-Bake Pumpkin Cheesecake

My oven gets a lot of action on Thanksgiving. Even days before The Big Day, it's making cornbread for the dressing, baking pie crusts, cooking rolls, etc. So having a super easy no-bake pumpkin cheesecake recipe to whip up is just what I'm after.

And it solves another little issue I have. I…errrr…well, I don't really love pumpkin pie. Don't hate me now! But you HAVE to have pumpkin pie on Thanksgiving, right? So, I like to make this one instead, because I actually like it (a lot!), and I don't have to take up valuable real estate in my oven to make it!

1 (8-ounce) package cream cheese, softened

1 (14-ounce) can pumpkin (not pie filling), divided

1 cup sugar (or to taste)

1 teaspoon vanilla extract

½ teaspoon pumpkin pie spice

Pinch of salt

1 (8-ounce) carton Cool Whip, thawed and divided

1 (9-inch) graham cracker pie crust

Whip cream cheese with an electric mixer until fluffy. Add about half the pumpkin, and continue mixing at medium speed until smooth.

Add remaining pumpkin, sugar, vanilla, pumpkin pie spice, and salt; mix well. Fold in about ⅔ of Cool Whip until evenly combined; spoon mixture into pie crust. Cover; chill 4 hours or until set.

Serve with remaining Cool Whip. Garnish with a sprinkle of pumpkin pie spice, if desired.

Makes 6–8 servings.

Banana Split Dessert

This dessert wraps up all the delicious ingredients of a classic banana split in one cool, creamy dessert. This is great to take to potlucks, because it travels beautifully!

2 cups graham cracker crumbs

1 stick butter, melted

1¼ cups sugar, divided

Pinch of salt

2 (8-ounce) packages cream cheese, softened

½ teaspoon vanilla extract

1 (16-ounce) carton Cool Whip, divided

3 bananas, sliced

1 (20-ounce) can crushed pineapple in heavy syrup, drained well

2 pints strawberries, sliced

Chopped nuts

Chocolate syrup

Maraschino cherries

Mix together graham cracker crumbs, melted butter, ¼ cup sugar, and salt; press into bottom of 9x13-inch baking dish. Bake at 350° for 10 minutes. Cool completely.

Beat cream cheese, vanilla, and remaining 1 cup sugar with an electric mixer until fluffy. Fold in 1 cup Cool Whip. Spread mixture evenly over crust.

Arrange banana slices over cream cheese mixture. Top with pineapple. Arrange strawberry slices over pineapple. Spread with remaining Cool Whip. (Make sure to go all the way to the edges to seal things up so the bananas don't brown.) Refrigerate 2 hours before serving.

To serve, sprinkle with nuts, drizzle with chocolate syrup, and top with cherries.

Makes 20–24 servings.

Peanut Butter Ripple Nutter Butter Banana Pudding

I think peanut butter can make anything taste better. I often melt peanut butter to drizzle over ice cream. It just adds a little something extra, and makes your kids think you're a rock star. Sometimes I like to drizzle a little on banana pudding, so I decided to make sort of a peanut butter banana pudding, using Nutter Butter cookies instead of vanilla wafers. And then I put layers of melted peanut butter in there that make two positively divine peanut butter ripples. Mercy!

1 (5.1-ounce) box vanilla or white chocolate instant pudding mix

2⅓ cups milk

⅔ cup creamy peanut butter

1 (1-pound package) Nutter Butter cookies

4–5 bananas, sliced

1 (8-ounce) tub Cool Whip, thawed

In a medium bowl or stand mixer, beat pudding mix and milk for 2 minutes; set aside.

Heat peanut butter in the microwave about 45 seconds, or until melted and pourable, stirring well after heating; set aside.

Arrange cookies in a single layer in the bottom of a square 2-quart dish. Pour half the pudding on top of cookies. Arrange a single layer of banana slices over pudding. Drizzle half the peanut butter over bananas. Spread half the Cool Whip over peanut butter. Repeat layers.

Cover; refrigerate 24 hours or until cookies are soft and cake-like. (It takes longer for Nutter Butters to soften up than it does vanilla wafers.)

Garnish with crushed Nutter Butter cookies. Serve with additional melted peanut butter, if desired.

Makes 10–12 servings.

Peanut Butter Ripple Nutter Butter Banana Pudding

Quick and Easy Banana Pudding

Y'all might want a divorce when I tell you this but...ugh...here goes—I like to make banana pudding with instant pudding. Can I come out from behind the couch now? Or are you still holding your flip-flop, ready to fling it at my head?

OK, let me explain. Do I like the taste of the homemade better? Yes, ma'am, I sure do. But I don't like what happens to the bananas when the warm pudding hits them. They turn grayish and kinda slimy. And if you let it cool first, it gets all gloppy and I don't like that, either. The trick is to add extra vanilla to the instant mix and use whole milk, and it's close enough to perfect for me!

2 (3.4-ounce) boxes vanilla instant pudding mix

3½ cups whole milk

1 teaspoon vanilla extract

40–50 vanilla wafers

4–5 bananas, sliced

1 (8-ounce) carton Cool Whip, thawed

Put pudding mix in a medium bowl; pour in milk and vanilla; beat for 2 minutes. Let mixture rest 1 minute, or until it begins to thicken.

Line bottom of 2-quart dish with vanilla wafers. Pour half pudding on top of cookies. Arrange a single layer of banana slices over pudding. Spoon half Cool Whip over bananas. Repeat layers, starting with cookies and ending with Cool Whip.

Cover, and refrigerate at least 6 hours or until cookies are soft and cake-like. Garnish with crushed vanilla wafers before serving, if desired.

Makes 12–20 servings.

Note:

I doubled this recipe to make the banana pudding pictured. If you want to make yours in a trifle dish like I did (with the cookies standing up like this), you'll need to double the recipe, too. Otherwise, just place cookies flat on the bottom of your dish.)

Traditional Homemade Banana Pudding

I'm including this traditional homemade version of banana pudding since I still make it when I want to put on the dog. You'll want to cook up this version if you're taking it to any family reunion south of the Mason-Dixon Line. Especially if it's your husband's family. Don't give your mother-in-law that kind of ammunition!

But feel free to take the easy route any other time, because I think it is absolutely delicious! Truly, I do! And, P.S....I think my mother-in-law would love it. But my MIL is Canadian, so I get off easy.

⅔ cup sugar

⅓ cup all-purpose flour

½ teaspoon salt

4 egg yolks

3 cups whole milk

1½ teaspoons vanilla extract

40–50 vanilla wafers

4–5 bananas, sliced

MERINGUE:

4 egg whites

¼ teaspoon cream of tartar

⅓ cup sugar

Combine sugar, flour, salt, egg yolks, and milk in top of a double boiler. Cook over boiling water, stirring constantly, until thickened, 10–14 minutes. Remove from heat; stir in vanilla.

Line bottom of 2-quart dish with vanilla wafers. Pour half the pudding on top of cookies. Arrange a single layer of banana slices over pudding. Repeat layers, starting with cookies and ending with bananas.

MERINGUE:

Put egg whites and cream of tartar in a bowl. Beat egg whites with a whisk attachment until foamy; gradually add sugar, and continue beating until stiff peaks form.

Spoon over top layer of bananas, going all the way to edge of dish to "seal" it. Place in oven, and broil on low until Meringue is lightly browned.

Cover; refrigerate at least 6 hours or until cookies are soft and cake-like.

Makes 10–12 servings.

So Easy Chocolate Éclair Dessert

We always called this "June's Dessert" growing up, because my Aunt June was the one who introduced us to this delicious creation! Aunt June made the chocolate topping from scratch, so that's the way I always made mine. I tried a similar dish at a potluck dinner one time, and couldn't get over how fantastic the chocolate topping was. I was shocked to learn that it was simply melted canned frosting! After that, there was no way I was going back to making mine from scratch. You won't be disappointed with this super luxurious dessert!

2 (3.4-ounce) boxes French vanilla instant pudding mix

3 cups whole milk

1 (16-ounce) carton Cool Whip, thawed

1 (14-ounce) box graham crackers

1 (16-ounce) can prepared chocolate fudge frosting

1 teaspoon vanilla extract

Mix pudding mixes with milk in a mixing bowl; beat for 2 minutes. Fold in Cool Whip until well combined.

Line bottom of 9x13-inch pan with graham crackers. Spread half of pudding mixture over crackers; top with another layer of graham crackers. Spread remaining half of pudding mixture over crackers; top with another layer of graham crackers. Press crackers down a bit so top is as flat and even as possible.

Microwave frosting at 50% power for 60 seconds. Add vanilla, and stir well; pour evenly over graham crackers. Cover, and refrigerate 3–4 hours, or until crackers are soft.

Makes 20–24 servings.

Blackberry Cobbler

Nanny lived on a dirt road and had a big ole bramble of wild blackberry bushes right by her driveway. She'd send me out with a quart-size Mason jar to pick berries whenever she wanted to cook up something sweet. I was taught at a young age to be mindful of snakes in places like that…so I wasn't too alarmed when a baby rattlesnake slithered by my bare foot. Being about eight years old at the time, I thought he was pretty neat, so I scooped him up, tossed him in my Mason jar and ran up to the house to show Nanny. Well, Nanny swept me, the jar, and that snake off the porch, and tried to knock me into next Tuesday with her straw broom. She told me to get back down the driveway and get her some blackberries, and if I ever tried to bring another serpent into her house, she'd whoop my behind! I believe she would have, too! Ever since that day I can't help but think of her and smile anytime I see blackberries.

6 cups fresh blackberries

1½ cups sugar (or less, if your berries are super sweet)

2 cups all-purpose flour

1 tablespoon baking powder

1 teaspoon salt

2 cups milk

2 sticks butter, melted

Combine blackberries and sugar in a large bowl; stir to coat berries with sugar. Cover, and let rest 30 minutes.

Combine flour, baking powder, and salt in a large bowl; stir well. Add milk and melted butter; stir until just combined. Pour batter into an ungreased 9x13-inch baking dish.

Gently spoon berries (with juice) evenly over batter, taking care not to stir. Bake at 375° for 1 hour, or until berries are bubbly and crust is golden brown. Cool for 20 minutes before serving.

Makes 20–24 servings.

Chocolate Cobbler

This is great to bring to a potluck or covered-dish dinner, because it doesn't have to be refrigerated. It always elicits "ooohs" and "ahhhhs" once someone spoons out that first serving and all that yummy fudgy sauce spills out all over the place!

¾ **cup sugar**

1 **cup all-purpose flour**

⅓ **cup cocoa powder**

2 **teaspoons baking powder**

½ **teaspoon salt**

½ **cup milk**

1⅓ **sticks butter, melted**

TOPPING:

¾ **cup sugar**

¼ **cup brown sugar**

¼ **cup cocoa powder**

Pinch of salt

1 **teaspoon vanilla extract**

1¼ **cups boiling water**

Combine sugar, flour, cocoa, baking powder, and salt in a small bowl; mix well, and set aside.

In a medium bowl, combine milk and melted butter. Add flour mixture; mix by hand or with an electric mixer until smooth (some small lumps are okay). Spread mixture into a shallow 2-quart baking dish or 9x9-inch baking pan (only metal pans will need to be greased).

TOPPING:

Combine sugar, brown sugar, cocoa, and salt in a small bowl; mix well. Sprinkle mixture evenly over base.

Add vanilla to boiling water; pour water slowly over sugar mixture. Do not stir.

Bake at 350° for 30–40 minutes, or until cobbler is nearly set in the middle. When you can really smell it, but there's still a little bit of wiggle in the very center, it's ready!

Cool 10–15 minutes. Serve warm, with vanilla ice cream for a special treat!

Makes 8–10 servings.

Chocolate Cobbler

Peanut Butter Stuffed Chocolate Crescent Rolls

One night my crew was itching for something sweet. So I started snooping around the pantry and all I came up with was a bag of mini chocolate chips. I considered making muffins but really wasn't up to dragging out the flour and the sugar and the baking powder and the milk and the…. So I opened up the fridge, hoping to find inspiration there, and spotted a can of crescent rolls.

A few globs of peanut butter and shakes of powdered sugar later, we were wolfing these things down like pros. They're best when they're still warm, but a few seconds in the microwave cures any leftovers just fine.

1 (8-count) can crescent rolls
½ cup peanut butter
¾ cup mini chocolate chips
Powdered sugar

Separate dough into the 8 perforated triangles. Spread 1 heaping tablespoon peanut butter onto wide end of each triangle (do not go all the way to the edges of the dough with the peanut butter or it will melt and ooze out all over the place).

Sprinkle chocolate chips evenly over dough. Roll each triangle per package instructions, starting with wide end. Place crescents 2 inches apart on a lightly buttered baking sheet. Bake at 375° for 9–11 minutes, or until light golden brown.

Remove from oven, and immediately sprinkle with powdered sugar. (To get that "bakery perfect" look with powdered sugar, use a mesh strainer or sifter, then tap the strainer against your hand over your target.)

Serve warm. Store any leftovers in an airtight container at room temperature, then slightly reheat in the microwave, if desired.

Makes 8 servings.

Index

About the Author

Mandy Rivers, an accomplished cook and food blogger, has parlayed her outgoing personality and cooking acumen into an unexpected success story.

In college, Mandy worked at a bona fide honky tonk in the middle of the Deep South, sometimes helping in their short-order kitchen. Once she got her feet wet, that was all it took! She became so enchanted with cooking, she soon started adding her own creations to the menu. It was there she realized she'd found two of her dearest passions: cooking and feeding people.

To catalog her award-winning recipes, and as a creative outlet, Mandy quietly started a food blog (www.SouthYourMouth.com) that became wildly successful overnight—due to her delicious, approachable recipes and hilarious personality.

The success of her blog was easily measured in the number of fans and followers on social media sites, like Pinterest, and it was there she caught the eye of the Food Network producers who were searching for the best cooks in America to star in the network series, *America's Best Cook*. Mandy was chosen to represent the South and compete in the premiere season of the latest sensation from Food Network.

Mandy's busy schedule includes a full-time job, marriage to "Husband," and three active children she calls her "onions." She enjoys creating new recipes and sharing them with family and friends. Mandy and her family live in Lexington, South Carolina.

Join Mandy now in her latest culinary accomplishment, *South Your Mouth Some More!* Read her entertaining insights and amusing stories while enjoying recipes that are sure to become your favorite go-to dishes for years to come.